REMAINING

A Sea Island's Journey

A Chronicle of the Landscape &
Political History of
Folly Beach, South Carolina
1972 – 1992

Richard L. Beck

HOME
HOUSE
PRESS

CHARLESTON, SOUTH CAROLINA

Remaining Folly: A Sea Island's Journey

Copyright © 2023 Richard L. Beck

ISBN: 978-1-952248-66-5 (trade paper)

ISBN: 978-1-952248-67-2 (eBook)

Published by:

H O M E
H O U S E
P R E S S

109 Broad St.
Charleston, SC 29401
www.homehousepress.com

Unless otherwise noted, all images appearing in this volume were provided by the author.

Printed in the USA.

This book is dedicated to

Rogers Oglesby
1929-2015

and all the members of the Folly Island Residents Association
who worked so hard to keep the soul and spirit of Folly
from being swept away.

*"A visionary is the one who sees things that are quite obvious,
much ahead of the rest."*

– Sandeep Shajpal –

Table of Contents

Acknowledgments vii

Abbreviations in *Remaining Folly* ix

A Note to Readers xi

Introduction: *The Role of the Charleston Harbor Jetties in Folly's History* 1

1 My Road to Folly 11

2 Scenes of Paradise with an Ocean View 21

3 Folly's Origin Story 41

4 Eastern Surfing Association v. City of Folly Beach 49

5 A Change Is Gonna Come 57

6 A Toe in the Water 59

7 National Attention, Local Chaos 61

8 How the Western Tip of Folly Island Became a County Park 67

9 Progress and Duplicity 79

10 Opponents 89

11 Losing the Dumbwaiter and Andre's Death 91

12 How to Win a War Without Winning a Battle 95

13 Good Deeds Punished 119

14 Renourishment: A Fifty-Year Commitment – 1978–1986 123

15 The 1988 Beachfront Management Bill – 1985–1990 133

16 The Final Straws 141

17 It's Not Over Till It's Over 149

18 Reflections 153

19 Déjà Vu All Over Again 155

Epilogue 163

APPENDIX

Resources 167

Cast of Characters 169

Acknowledgments

As I sit down to thank the people who helped me with this book, I am struck by the realization that, while writing a book does demand a lot of time spent alone, in the end, it is a collaborative effort that brings the author into relationship with a wonderful new universe of people.

First of all, I'd like to thank my wife Karen for her patience during all the time I was literally and figuratively absent while working on this project. She is my rock.

I would also like to thank Cookie Jamison Bragg, the widow of Jack Wilbanks, for her generosity in making Jack's files and images available so that I could tell the story of the formative years of Folly's politics for the first time. My thanks go out to Rita Oglesby for making Rogers's notes available so that I could better understand his contributions and traumas. I was fortunate to have access to the material on Folly's early history that Dinos Liollio had gathered in completing his master's thesis.

A special thank you to Folly's coastal engineer, Dr. Nicole Elko, for making sure that my narrative on the history of the Charleston harbor jetties is accurate.

What started as a collection of stories would not have become a book without the help of my writers' group. I joined Mary Johnston's Wordworks writing group, and began my education in the craft of writing by Mary, Rob Turkewitz, Anne Combes, Stuart Ames, and Ken Ryan. With their help, I was able to turn those stories into a book that, hopefully, is both interesting and enjoyable.

I would like to thank my beta readers, Ben Peeples, Sarah King, Ken Ryan, and Lynn Butler, for taking the time to study an unfinished work and provide insight into its readability and its need for improvement. Beta readers make the first "final" draft of a manuscript possible.

Ben Peeples served as Folly's city attorney for forty years. I'd like to thank him for our conversations about Folly's history. Ben was an insider with a different perspective and can not only recall events, but can also punctuate recollections with funny stories. His memory was invaluable to the telling of stories of so long ago truthfully.

I believe that everyone who attempts to write a book is comforted by the E. B. White's admonition, "The best writing is rewriting." After 100 or so drafts, it's the help of a professional editor that makes it all come together. I would like to thank Mary Johnston for having the experience to patiently guide me through the editing process. There is no way that you would be holding this book without her skills.

Thank you, Cyrus Martin of Rhodes Editorial for helping me get unstuck when neither Mary nor I could feel comfortable with a portion of the book.

This book contains a large number of images. Coordinating the cataloging of those images, managing the captions, and keeping track of the proposed position of those images in the manuscript is a job that requires a special kind of expertise. Thank you, Cassandra Foster.

In closing, I would like to thank my publishing team, Tom Tisdale and Vally Sharpe of Home House Press. Making the commitment to have someone turn your work into something that can be shared with pride is an important decision. I am blessed to have been supported by the Home House Press team. Vally is invaluable as a professional editor, book designer, and publisher. From our first contact, she was professional, available, and fun every time we faced the question of which path to choose.

Thank you all.

Richard L. Beck, DMD

Abbreviations in *Remaining Folly*

AFDC   Aid to Families with Dependent Children
CHNP   Charleston Harbor Navigation Project
CTAR   Charleston Trident Real Estate Association
DHEC   Department of Health and Environmental Control (State of S.C.)
FIRA   Folly Island Resident's Association
FRA   Folly Resident's Association
FSBPA   Florida Shore and Beach Preservation
FU   Folly United
ISTRs   Investor-owned short-term rentals
NSF   National Science Foundation
OCRM   Office of Coastal Resource Management
PRC   Charleston County Parks and Recreation Commission
PRD   Planned Residential Development
P&Z   Planning and Zoning Commission
RPAC   Real Estate Political Action Committee (National)
SFF   Save Folly's Future
SFR   Single family residential
SCBMB   South Carolina Beachfront Management Bill of 1988
SCPRT   South Carolina Parks, Recreation and Tourism Commission
SCSBPA   South Carolina Shore and Beach Preservation Association
SLED   State Law Enforcement Division
TIA   Transient Ischemic Attack

A Note to Readers

Although the quirky little beach town that you see when you drive onto Folly today is certainly changed from the Folly of the 1970s and 1980s, in crucial ways, Folly has not changed at all.

Unlike the Folly of forty-five years ago, the town is now booming. Tourist season never ends, thanks partly to a sixty-five percent population increase in Charleston County over the last forty years, heavy promotion mandated by the accommodation tax revenue system and, most important, the benefits of a successful periodic beach renourishment program.

Periodic renourishment has completely changed the face of the oceanfront from one of distress to one of desirability. Heading to the beach in the 1980s required that visitors consult a tide chart because, at high tide, there was very little or no dry sand beach. Today, two rows of sand dunes stand between the high-tide line and many of the shoreline homes—a striking contrast to the earlier homeowners' desperate and ineffective attempts to keep the ocean from destroying those same homes four decades ago. This shoreline stability has changed the perception of the community from one that was to be avoided to one that is in demand. Money and the changes it brings are flowing to Folly.

Yet, despite all the improvements, if you take the time to look more closely, you will see that its intrinsic identity, the "Folly-ness" of the town, remains.

Folly is still the same small scale, environmentally sensitive, and inclusive community that it was in 1975 when I rented my first beachfront cottage. The churches, bars, shops, restaurants, library, and post office still occupy the same buildings that housed similar businesses. Community-based organizations like the churches, the Civic Club, the Exchange Club the Garden Club, and Turtle Watch still thrive. Only one building is over four stories tall, and except for a compact business district, Folly is still a single-family residential community. Buildings are still small enough that they show respect for human scale without stunting minds or chilling spirits.

Why has Folly changed so much and yet so little?

It is interesting that, never having enjoyed the cache and stability of Sullivan's, Kiawah, or Isle of Palms, Folly has avoided succumbing to the financial forces that so often homogenize and overdevelop beachfront communities. It's especially interesting if you know that the Comprehensive Land Use and Zoning Update that Folly adopted in 1977 projected a completely different Folly Beach than we see today. All the planning stars were aligned for Folly to become just one more completely commercialized, high rise, high-density beach community—another K-Mart by the sea.

Having served in Folly's government those many years ago, I can tell you that the look and feel of present-day Folly is not the result of random chance. Plans to completely commercialize the community were thwarted because of hard-won victories by residents who battled an onslaught of developers (supported by a pro-development City Council) for the soul of the community. And those battles were won under an exceptional set of circumstances.

I was prompted to begin writing this book in 2012 by the celebration of the fortieth anniversary of Folly's incorporation. Seven former mayors—Regas Kennedy, Lavern James, me, Rex Whitcomb, Bob Linville, Vernon Knox—and current mayor, Tim Goodwin, were all present.

Each mayor gave a review of his years in office, all of which I had observed. As I listened, I realized how much more complex the reality of those years was from what was being presented as Folly's history. While every other mayor seemed satisfied with a brief description of his experience, I came away unfulfilled. It was especially painful for me to be so brief because I knew that the context of my eleven years of service was unique, complicated, and fundamental to preserving the physical nature and feel of the Folly we know today.

I was reminded that institutional memory is fleeting in today's world and that without a written record, images, conversations, names, friends, opponents, victories, losses, implications, loves, motives, and circumstances are simply forgotten in the final closing of a pair of eyes.

As I thought more about the importance of preserving Folly's history, I decided to document both the overall history of Folly and the important political events that would impact it in order to give an accurate picture of this particular sea island's journey through time.

Like all good histories, this book weaves together several stories. It tells the story of the environmental forces that shaped the history of the island. The changes in the beachfront of Folly and the story of the events in Folly's journey have to be understood together.

The history of the politics of the period of Folly's incorporation in 1972 and the events that shaped the next twenty years are crucial to an understanding of Folly's present. The story of the extraordinary community activism of that period makes for an instructive and memorable tale—its relevance growing as the pressures to change the character of the community grow with every passing year. I want to introduce the people that were personally and spiritually invested in the outcome of the struggles of that time.

It is also my goal to provide an insider's look into the behind-the-scenes dynamics of Folly's heritage—the story of a small beach town that by the 1970s had fallen out of favor with the larger Charleston community—an account of the lifestyle and opportunities that this isolation nurtured, and the relationship of that lifestyle to Folly's enduring character.

I believe that these two decades, 1972–1992, set in motion forces and included decisions that, in a very real sense, made this time period the most formative years of modern Folly's history.

How Folly became and remained Folly is the tale I want to tell.

Notes on style

I often use the personal pronoun "I" for the sake of economy; some decisions and actions were mine alone, whereas others were the result of consensus. I use the pronoun "we" for the same reason. By "we" or "us," I mean all of the people with whom I collaborated to accomplish a particular objective.

I use "The City of Folly Beach," "Folly," "Folly Island," and "Folly Beach" interchangeably.

Where I record an event as a conversation in quotes, I was either present or am depicting the event through the eyes of participants whom I trust. All dialogue used has been reviewed by at least one of the actual participants.

Although I may not always describe the people who were important to specific events, I have tried my best to include their names to preserve them in that event's context.

This narrative covers most events chronologically, though in several instances, notable events happened simultaneously through certain periods of Folly's history. In these cases, I recount them separately for the sake of clarity. I will occasionally refer to an earlier period when I feel the added context is important for the reader's understanding. I will also extend an event's history up to the present day if I think it will be of interest to the reader.

Because the community was sharply divided on the issues of the time, it is a foregone conclusion that my viewpoint will not be shared by everyone who was politically active between 1972 and 1992. Yet, while this book *does* represent my perspective, I have tried my best to provide a factually accurate and balanced record of the politics and influential events of those years.

In the opening chapters, I tell the more personal story of how I came to Folly as a young man—and why I fell in love with it—and then move quickly to how I became involved in the political growing pains of a community newly responsible for its own destiny.

It is my intent that this work will motivate others to record and add their own stories to the rich tapestry that is Folly Island's history. I hope you will find it interesting, informative, and enjoyable.

But first, I think it important to discuss the issue that is at the very center of Folly's story and the cause of the greatest challenges that it has faced on its journey—not in 1972, but over a century ago.

Let's begin.

REMAINING

Folly

Introduction

The Role of the Charleston Harbor Jetties in Folly's History

The Charleston Harbor jetties, which were completed in 1896. Quincy A. Gilmore, Union commander of the siege of Charleston, was the chief engineer.

It is impossible to understand Folly's overall history and its politics during my time in office without understanding the damaging effect that the creation of the Charleston Harbor Navigation Project (CHNP) had on the shorelines of Morris and Folly Islands. The changes in the beach at Folly and the history of the political events of the 1980s are inseparable.

Just how the CHNP influenced Folly's evolution is complicated. I will begin with an explanation of how tides, sand, and wind interplay to shape the coast. Let's start at the entrance to the harbor of the settlement the colonists called Charles Towne. Take a minute to look at the map on the following page from the time of the British blockade of Charleston in 1780. Dated just 100 years out from the founding the city, the map depicts the conditions of the harbor entrance that are not materially different from those that the first colonists found in April 1670.

Map of Charleston Harbor, 1780. *Boston Public Library*

As this map indicates, the entrance to the main ship channel for Charleston Harbor and the 1768 colonial lighthouse were south of the harbor proper. The approach to this channel was guarded by a series of offshore sand shoals. More accurate navigation maps from the time of the Civil War depict these shoals, indicated by the shaded areas in the ocean, as three to five miles long, stretching from the middle of Sullivan's Island south past the "washout" on Folly Island.

From 1670 until the turn of the 20th century, mariners had to wait for the effects of wind and tide to allow their sailing ships to cross the ever-changing outer bar and enter the main ship channel, make a hard-right, sail the entire length of Morris Island, almost to Sullivan's Island, in a channel of varying width and depth, and then make a left turn into Charleston Harbor. The impediment that the "bar" imposed even got a mention in *A Diary from Dixie*, Mary Chesnut's diary. On or about April 12, 1861, the official start of the Civil War, Mary wrote, "The war steamers are still there, outside the bar. And there are people who thought the Charleston bar 'no good' to Charleston. The bar is the

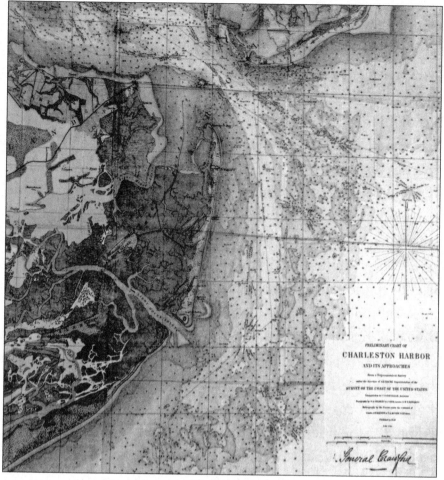

Navigational Chart for Charleston Harbor 1863
Library of Congress

silent partner or sleeping partner, and in this fray, it is doing yeoman service."

The problems with navigability didn't stop Charleston from becoming one of the most important ports in colonial America, but there was always a need to make the channel not only straighter but deeper and more predictable. To that end, the Charleston Harbor Navigation Project (CHNP) was completed in the summer of 1895.

Designed and constructed by the U.S. Army Corps of Engineers at the request of the city fathers of Charleston, the project consisted of two continuous walls of sofa-sized granite blocks that defined the borders of a new, more predictable entrance channel. The north jetty started on the western one-third of Sullivan's Island and curved out into the ocean, for some 15,443 feet (2.9 miles). The south jetty started on the east end of Morris Island and was similarly curved for a length of 19,104 feet (3.6 miles). Together they formed a funnel that concentrated the more efficient outgoing tide into a jet of water that naturally scoured and straightened the channel. The original design was to create a no-maintenance depth of twenty-one feet. The dredged depth today approaches 60 feet.

While the new jetty system ensured a more predictable entrance to the harbor, there were unintended consequences. The jetties altered the currents and physically blocked the normal flow of beach sand along the coast. The combination of these changes had a devastating effect on the islands to the south of the new main ship channel which, of course, included Folly.

How did these jetties cause so much damage? Well, a river of sand (littoral sand transport) flows along South Carolina's coast; it is generated by the northeasterly winds, which cause a strong current that moves sand along the coast from north to south. This movement of sand is interrupted at the inlets between our sea islands by the currents of the more dominant outgoing tide, an interruption that causes sand to collect just offshore and form an offshore delta, also called an ebb tidal sand bar. These sandbars are typical of every inlet on South Carolina's coast.

This river of sand crosses the many inlets on our coast by a process called bar bypassing. (See the chart facing page.) The sand flowing south builds up on the north side of a channel (stage 1) and shifts the channel to the south (stage 2). This extension eventually becomes unstable, and usually during some event that causes an unusually big tide, the outgoing tide will break through the weakest point of the extension of the shoal, reorienting the channel to the north. This reorientation releases the sand held in the shoal to bypass the channel, move onshore to the next island, and continue its journey south (stage 3). The jetties blocked this process and cut of the flow of sand from the north to Morris and Folly islands.

The next image gives a true-to-scale perspective of the size of the jetties and the extent of shoreline change they caused. The jetties

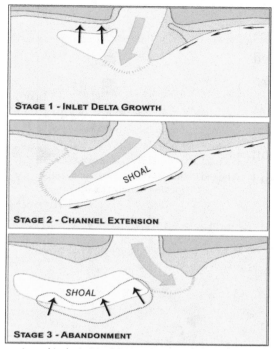

STAGE 1 - INLET DELTA GROWTH

STAGE 2 - CHANNEL EXTENSION

SHOAL

STAGE 3 - ABANDONMENT

SHOAL

A graphic depiction of the bar-bypassing process. 1977
Hubbard. *Reused by permission, Elko et al., 2020*

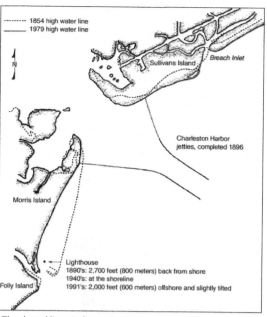

...... 1854 high water line
—— 1979 high water line

Sullivans Island   Breach Inlet

Charleston Harbor
jetties, completed 1896

Morris Island

Lighthouse
1890's: 2,700 feet (800 meters) back from shore
1940's: at the shoreline
1991's: 2,000 feet (600 meters) offshore and slightly tilted

Folly Island

The dotted lines indicate the position of the shoreline in 1854;
the solid lines indicate the shoreline position 125 years later
in 1979. Sullivan's Island grew, Morris Island shrank, and the
second Charleston Light, built in 1876, found itself offshore.
From *An Illustrated History of Tidal Inlet Changes in South
Carolina*, by Gary A. Zarillo, Larry G. Ward, and Miles O. Hayes.
Reused by permission.

trapped sand for Sullivan's Island and caused growth. They blocked the movement of sand to Morris and Folly islands and caused erosion.

The existence of the jetties and the dredging of the entrance channel to Charleston Harbor combined to make it impossible for the sand that would normally have travelled along the coast to make it past the modified entrance to Charleston Harbor. Deprived of the input of new sand, Morris Island eroded. A 1983 US Army Corps of Engineers' Phase II interim report titled "Historical Bathymetric Change and Shoreline Movement in the Vicinity of Charleston Harbor" estimated that Morris Island lost 955 acres of high land between 1900 and 1983. The current Morris Island Lighthouse was 2,700 feet from the surf when its light shone for the first time on October 1, 1876. By 1937, the ocean had reached the lighthouse and the keeper's quarters. The site was deemed unsafe and all the buildings were either removed or destroyed in 1938. The lighthouse was protected by a surrounding cofferdam of steel and was automated. The Morris Island Lighthouse, Charleston's second lighthouse, was retired from duty and abandoned when the Sullivan's Island Lighthouse first shone on June 15, 1962.

The photos below are a pictorial review of the effect of erosion on Morris Island and the Morris Island Lighthouse.

The Old Charleston Light compound, 1883. *Charleston County Library.*

The Morris Island Lighthouse in 1937. Courtesy of Katherine Davis Craig.

Morris Island Lighthouse, 1999.
Taken by Larry Workman

Morris Island Lighthouse, 2021.

Between the 1920s and the 1940s, Folly's beaches were wide enough to park two lines of cars above the tideline. The beautiful wide sand beach, just a couple of steps lower than the level of Center Street, had largely disappeared by the mid-1950s.

In the 1980s, when the erosion committee was trying to measure shoreline recession on Folly, there was no historical information

An aerial view of Folly in the late 1940s. *Wilbanks collection.*

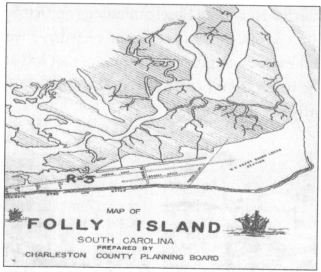

A 1966 planning map for the township of Folly that shows Benket and Sumter Drives as platted. Both streets were built on the beach oceanward of East Ashley in 1962. By the early 1970s, the streets had been lost to erosion.

available for most of the length of Folly, but the city's coastal engineering consultant, Eric Olsen, PE, estimated that between 1898 and the 1980s, over 250 million cubic yards of sand had been lost from the sand resources that kept the beach at Folly healthy.

The beaches at Folly actually did well for several decades after the jetties were built as the old entrance channel sandbars and Morris Island eroded and provided sand to Folly's beaches, but as those two sources were dispersed, the flow of sand to Folly diminished. And the size and quality of Folly's beach suffered. The first timber groins, built perpendicular to the beach to try slow erosion, were built in 1949.

A deteriorated groin.

By the time that Hurricane Hazel came along on October 14, 1954, the area around the end of Center Street was protected by a wooden seawall. Hazel served the knockout punch for the ramp that had allowed cars to drive onto the beach from Center Street. The ramp was replaced by a stairway shortly after the storm.

Damage to the automobile ramp from Hurricane Hazel in 1954, looking east and west. *Wilbanks collection.*

Erosion affected the east end of Folly Island first. As the ocean reached their residences, homeowners scrambled to throw something, anything, between their homes and the encroaching ocean. Old cars, concrete and rebar from construction demolition, sidewalks and curbing from highway demolition, various engineered solutions, wooden bulkheads, concrete bulkheads, worn out tires, rock revetments, Christmas trees, bales of hay—you name it, and it was on Folly's beaches. With little or no agreement among neighbors about what, if any method of protection would be used, Folly's shoreline became a mishmash of uncoordinated efforts to control erosion. It was both an ugly and ineffective way to preserve the structures and made the beach less usable.

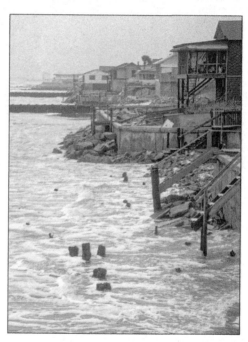

East 4th Street looking west.
(Note the tree stumps on the beach.)

When I moved to Folly in the mid-1970s, there was only a small dry sand beach at high tide for much of the length of the island. By the mid-1980s, pine roots from a time when mature trees grew beyond what we knew to be the edge of the ocean were exposed. Folly hired contractors to take tractors out onto the beach and remove the stumps.

Erosion had progressed to the point that the beach at Folly had become a liability. Real estate values fell to the lowest on the east coast. Folly's reputation in the larger Charleston community became one of an undesirable, rundown, absentee-owned, and drug-infested oddity. Folly had lost its appeal as a shore destination and its community adapted to the slower pace that occurs when demand drops to an all-time low; it was quiet on Folly in the 1970s and 1980s. This downtrodden Folly is the Folly I came to love.

The beach around the Atlantic House, 1982.

1

My Road to Folly

I was born on the peninsula of Charleston in the mid-1940s and grew up on James Island in Riverland Terrace in the 1950s and 60s, a top contender for the most uncorrupted of all settings. As a ten-year-old, I could take my eight-year-old brother, Carl, into Charleston on the Riverland Terrace bus line, watch a movie at the Garden Theatre on King Street, and catch the bus at the corner of Calhoun and King for the return ride back to Stono Shores Road and a short walk home. No one thought anything of it. There was no danger. The greatest fear we Beck boys faced was that our mother would use our first *and* middle names when she called out for us.

Sears and Roebuck on Calhoun Street had the only escalator in the county. People were attracted to King Street so they could ride it and enjoy the air conditioning, which was absent from many of our homes. Downtown Charleston was the commercial hub of the community—King Street was one way from Spring Street south, all the way to the Battery. Buster Brown shoes from Condon's Department Store were the best shoes to own because their good sturdy leather soles allowed the clamps on our metal-wheeled skates an unfailing grip. The clerk always showed our mother how well the shoes fit our feet by irradiating them and making the green display of our foot bones available to her for her final approval. (In the 1950s, radiation was thought to be benign...)

I distinctly remember the first time King's Highway (now Riverland Drive) was paved with asphalt instead of the traditional mixture of tar and small rounded pebbles called macadam, because we no longer had to go all the way to Riverland Terrace Elementary School to skate. Now we could skate on the highway.

At Lowder's Grocery, Mrs. Lowder would begrudgingly give us credit for the two-cent deposit on each discarded soda bottle in the wagon full of bottles that my friend Ricky Croucher and I had collected in the ditches on the way to her store. Our newfound wealth was transformed into a bag of candy before we left the store.

When I was twelve years old, my Columbia bicycle from Robinson's Bicycle Shop at the corner of King and Ann Streets served two purposes: allowing me to slip the surly bonds of earth and to deliver the Charleston Evening Post to my 72 customers on Woodland Shores Road.

For a time, my mother's older sister Dickie was married to Mr. Bill Strickland, who was at one time or another, a Burger Beer truck driver, city marshal, and a bar owner on Folly.

My aunt and uncle lived above their bar. Occasionally, she took me to the beach to spend the weekend with her. I clearly remember that Center Street ended in a ramp that allowed cars to drive onto the beach. Pictures of the beachfront from that era show a mini-carnival complete with a Ferris wheel. I remember riding the bumper cars and the intoxicating fragrance of cotton candy blending with the aromas of hot dog chili, creosote pilings, and salt air.

While I went to the beach and even played in bands on the pier in the mid-1960s, I have no stories of a childhood on Folly Beach because

A view from the beach at the end of Center Street in the early 1950s. *Wilbanks collection.*

the beach was not my choice for water fun. I was a river rat and spent my time waterskiing from a small sand beach at the foot of the 1952 version of the Stono River Bridge with my mom and dad and my three brothers, Charlie, Carl, and Jimmy.

I went to grammar school and high school on James Island. The community was so small that I graduated from high school with the same people I started the first grade with. Few people moved here and no one seemed to move away.

After graduating from Erskine College in 1968 and the MUSC School of Dental Medicine in 1972, I worked in public health as the director of a program that provided mobile dental care to six- to twelve-year-old children who qualified for Aid for Dependent Children (AFDC) assistance at the eleven outlying elementary schools of Pickens County in northwestern South Carolina.

I spent two years in Pickens. I loved my job and my patients, and while those two years were idyllic, there was no salt water to be found in the upstate. I missed the Lowcountry and Charleston.

I was asked to write a grant application to duplicate the Pickens program in Charleston. When the grant was funded, I returned to my hometown.

Although the new clinic got me back to Charleston, the upper management of the program turned out to be toxic and unprofessional. Frustrated by the poor coordination of our patient care and weary of being admonished for not being a team player, I lost confidence and became depressed—to the point of being suicidal. One night, out of the blue, I got a call from a dear friend, Geraldine Harper. After talking for a couple of minutes, she stopped me. "Richard, you don't sound right," she said. "Is everything okay?"

I paused and took advantage of the opportunity to be truthful. "I am completely miserable and don't know what I am going to do."

She patiently listened to my story and then asked me a simple question. "Why don't you quit?"

I was pitiful. "Could I? What would I do?"

"Jesus! Wake up, Richard. You're a dentist! Get a grip! You can do anything you want to do. Go in tomorrow morning, give them your notice, take some time off, and then decide what you want to do next."

That conversation redirected my life. I resigned the next day but didn't feel better. In fact, I felt more like a failure than ever. I was stuck—and getting unstuck would take some doing.

Moving forward

When I resigned in July 1975, I was 28 years old and had been riding motorcycles for three years. After my resignation, I picked up a book—*Zen and the Art of Motorcycle Maintenance* by Robert M. Pirsig. For me—a lover of motorcycles, a nut about maintenance, and a dabbler in Buddhism—the title was perfect.

The book is about a motorcycle ride that the main character takes with his son and two friends after being released from a psychiatric hospitalization—part narrative of a cross-country motorcycle ride, part handbook about the spiritual aspects of motorcycle maintenance, part insight into the narrator's descent into insanity, and part examination of the nature of rationality itself. The book had a profound impact on me. Couple that with the fact that the 1969 movie **Easy Rider** was still fresh in my mind, and not surprisingly, I envisioned a motorcycle trip as my road back to clarity.

I decided that I would ride across the country on my motorcycle and set September 1 as my departure date. Great idea, but I was the only rider without a regular schedule and could find no one to go with me. My younger brother, Carl, expressed an interest in buying a bike and going, but I hesitated because he had no motorcycle experience. In addition, my mother had taken me aside and threatened me with the severance of our relationship if I took my younger, more headstrong brother with me and he ended up mangled in a ditch somewhere. I would go by myself.

Two days before my departure date, my three brothers and their significant others had a going away party for me, but it wasn't a party to give me a hearty sendoff as you might imagine. No, they hoped to persuade me not to go by telling me stories of all the people they had ever known or heard of who had been maimed or killed on a motorcycle.

During the course of the evening, Carl decided he was going with me. His girlfriend said he was definitely *not* going. After listening to them argue for several minutes, I turned to my little brother and said, "Listen, I'm leaving at 8:00 on Monday morning. If you're going, be there at eight, or I'll see you when I get back." Carl rode up at the appointed time on an obviously abused and neglected motorcycle he had bought the night before and said, "Let's do it."

So it was that we set off on a cross-country motorcycle odyssey on Labor Day of 1975. For six weeks, I had the wind in my face, stark reality six inches from my feet, and ten hours a day to sing as loud as I wanted to.

Do it yourself therapy

Riding a motorcycle all day, every day, in the varied conditions of a cross-country ride has powerful therapeutic value. The passage of time seems to slow to a crawl and perceptions are sharpened. Unlike riding in a car, on a motorcycle you are part of the scene—not watching it. The intimacy I felt with my surroundings created indelible images in my mind that are as crystal clear today as they were 47 years ago.

All of my attention was in the moment. Each stretch of highway had its own smells, its own sense of warmth or chill, its own humidity, its own air clarity, its own angle of sunlight. Carl and I had no schedule. We had the luxury of unlimited time, and with it came a sense of freedom and calm.

Whether we were riding through the Appalachian Mountains, crossing the Mississippi River, seeing the beauty of the Ozarks, or feeling the constant crosswind in the ride across Kansas, we marveled at our country's expanse. When we reached the Rockies, we were in a landscape that was both so foreign and beautiful that our sense of wonder was elevated beyond anything we could have hoped for. We simply could not believe our good fortune and hooted out loud as we leaned into each flowing curve on the profoundly beautiful ride northwest from Pueblo, Colorado on US 50 that crosses the Royal George and then follows the course of the Arkansas River all the way to the turn off to Independence Pass. Crossing this pass on a motorcycle in a snow shower is something that I will never forget. Utah introduced us to otherworldly rock formations and Nevada to a new motorcycle companion, Brandon, who was traveling by bike, with two couples in a van on a cross-country adventure of their own. As our caravan continued west, Carl and I became detached from everything but the adventure.

The wonders continued to unfold when we arrived at Yosemite at midnight and set up camp in the freezing cold, rode across the San Francisco Bay Bridge, and were spellbound by the ride on the Coast Highway south from Monterey. Farther down the coast, we camped next to a California couple who were generous enough to share their cannabis, and I had my first experience with sinsemilla while camping amongst the redwoods at Big Sur. When we turned east, we sat on the beach as the day ended and then watched the sunset for the second time in one day from the hills above San Luis Obispo.

Forty miles east of Bakersfield, California, deep into the Mojave Desert, Carl's bike suffered a total electrical failure. We were rescued by an electrical engineer who worked at White Sands Proving Grounds. He diagnosed and rewired the bike in less than twenty minutes. Being on the road on a motorcycle will teach you to believe in miracles.

As Carl and I rode back across the country, our funds ran low, so if the weather turned bad, motels were no longer an option. We would pull into our last town of the day, take the first right, and ride until we found a secluded spot for our tent. Most nights it was dark by the time we stopped, so we couldn't be sure of the safety of our surroundings. One morning, outside of Albuquerque, New Mexico, we were awakened by the foremen of a road construction crew, who advised us that in about ten minutes we would not be very happy with our campsite. We had camped in an interstate construction site about fifty yards from the earth-moving equipment.

Carl's bike then developed mechanical issues which changed our travel pattern and forced our ten-hour travel days farther and farther into darkness. Our last several nights on the road, we spent way too many hours of white-knuckled attention countering the air turbulence of the tractor trailers we passed on the dark and rain-soaked stretches of I-40 East.

In living through this—and I can't say where or when because there were so many beautiful, terrifying, and reassuring moments on that ride—my sense of time softened as did the sense of my place in it. I felt my strength and resolve return. I returned to myself again and remembered who I had been before I lost my confidence.

By the time we got back to Charleston, Carl and I were all but broke, and I was unemployed. I needed a cheap place to stay. Fortunately, a dental school classmate, Dr. Steve Ray, had a summer rental beach house on Folly Beach he would rent me for the winter for $100/month. (In the winter months it was vacant because it was impossible to heat.) I moved into 704 East Arctic in mid-October of 1975, and soon developed a genuine fondness for this little island community.

On my journey, I also decided to go into practice for myself. When I got settled in, I contacted the dental equipment suppliers about any practice opportunities available. A short time later, a professional office space opened up on James Island at 914 Folly Road and my attention became focused on starting my practice, which I accomplished on January 12, 1976. I was excited to be in control of my destiny again and to be starting my career in my home town.

About 18 months later, Mr. Fred Adams came in for a dental visit. I was aware that Fred was the mayor of Folly in 1976. When he asked me how I liked Folly, I told him how much I enjoyed living there and that I planned to buy a home on the island. As we walked to the front desk, Fred said something that would change my life. "You seem to have a real love for the community. Have you ever thought about running for office on Folly?" When I assured him I hadn't, he continued. "Folly needs some young people like you to get involved. Think about it." He paused and added, "I'll help you if you decide to run."

Although my journey into politics technically started with that conversation, the decision to run was rooted in my love for Folly, which began the day I set foot in my four-room summer rental on the edge of the Atlantic Ocean.

704 East Arctic, 1975

"Coffee at the Old Sanitary, Folly Beach, SC"

 This watercolor of the interior of the Sanitary Restaurant, which for forty years occupied the building next to what will soon be Coconut Joe's, was painted by artist Karen Tempel in about 1990. With Karen's permission, I have included it in this book because it captures the unpretentious charm of both this wonderful restaurant and the essence of the Folly community during the years I am writing about.

 This watercolor takes us back in time. Lottie, Eleanor, Rachel and Martha Harvey provided comfort food in an atmosphere of soothing colors. People were so at home there that it took at least ten minutes to leave because everyone knew everyone else. The red and white linoleum floors, the simple wooden benches without cushions, the plastic flowers, the local art, the thick ceramic coffee cups, sandwiches named after members of the community—these provided the sacred familiarity that makes a community home.

 Folly was our place of respite. We loved it enough to defend it.

Chapter 2

Scenes of Paradise with an Ocean View

In the two years that passed between my moving to Folly and my running for office, I fell deeply in love with the place. As the years unfolded, that attachment only deepened.

I remember a little about the Folly of my childhood. In the 1950s and 1960s, there were many proper homes there, but it was also possible to find an old school bus or a camper precariously balanced on a cinder block foundation, being used as a second home. The septic systems of such domiciles were often fifty-five-gallon drums stuck in a hole in the ground, ventilated with an axe, and surrounded by oyster shells. Winter rentals were rare.

From the 1930s to 1950s, a ramp at the end of Center Street allowed cars to drive directly onto the beach. The ramp was damaged during Hurricane Hazel in 1954 and then lost forever when a 1,700-foot concrete seawall was placed as a part of the development of the ill-fated Folly Beach Ocean Plaza in 1960.

In the 1970s, access to the beach was still there, but by then it was a dangerous pedestrian stairway that ended in the surf at high tide. Erosion had lowered the level of the beach and made safe access to the beach from Center Street all but impossible.

By the late 1970s, the structures behind the seawall were badly deteriorated as each successive owner's intent to revitalize the area was foiled by the increasing danger of the surf at the base of the seawall and the poor quality of the beach island-wide.

Blacky's Campground (now Little Oak Island) was more or less a squatter settlement loosely administered by a local character called "Cap'n Blacky." In this semi-autonomous world, people established long-term seasonal camping sites within the boundaries of their "property." It was not unusual to have fifty to sixty campsites in active use on the twelve-acre island.

Until the early 1970s, the Folly Dance Pier was usually busy. It had a history as a venue for entertainment that dated back to the late 1930s—including the early rock and rollers. In my era, the pier hosted the likes of the Tams, Curtis Mayfield, the Chairmen of the Board, the Swingin' Medallions, Bill Pinckney and the Drifters, Fats Domino, Wilson Picket, Hank Ballard and the Midnighters, Frankie Valli, Doug Clark and the Hot Nuts, as well as Maurice Williams and the Zodiacs. People danced the Jerk, the Boogaloo, the Twist, the Hustle, the Pony, the Funky Chicken, the Mashed Potato, and the Dog. The Shag, the most durable and popular dance, was well on its way to becoming the South Carolina State Dance in 1984. The state motto, "Dum Spiro Spero" was commonly translated, "If you don't shag—you ain't SH#%."

The pier had a large raised stage facing the ocean on its north end and a long bar along its west side. There were plenty of tables and chairs and a parquet dance floor for showing off your stuff. Most of the area's local bands looked forward to a night playing on the pier—the sounds of the surf beneath your feet, the crowd noise, the motion of the building as the breakers rounded its pilings, and the energy of the loosely controlled chaos of that place all combined to make the Folly Pier unique.

The popularity of the dance pier waned as the condition of the beach worsened and the island's popularity decreased. The deterioration of the quality of the beach in the 1970s and the attendant decline in the quality of the housing stock caused Folly to fall out of favor as a place to visit. Erosion changed the once thriving recreation resource with a thriving business community into a sleepy coastal backwater.

It seemed that the only people who loved Folly were its residents and the old-timers that maintained their rental cottages. Sometimes, though, a curse is a blessing in disguise. The blessing to Folly was that the community was unmolested by the constraints and commotion too much attention brings. It was quiet and relaxed. Housing and food were cheap. From September through May, we had the bars and restaurants to ourselves, easy access to Charleston, and a manageable number of visitors in the summer.

In the 1970s and 1980s, the light at Camp Road and Folly Road was the last stoplight before the one at Center Street and Ashley Avenue. There were no traffic jams on Folly, and you could park almost anywhere for free.

When you drove onto Folly, the horizon that indicated America's eastern edge opened up to you at the end of Center Street. There was so little traffic that its one traffic light became a flashing signal on the Tuesday after Labor Day. The next weekend, the locals would gather to have an impromptu we-have-it-to-ourselves-again party. You could almost get away with taking a nap on Center Street on a February day.

Until the late 1960s, Dennis McKevlin's Bowling Alley at the corners of East Arctic and Center Street had hinged openings at chest height on the Arctic and Center Street sides that allowed patrons to enjoy the sidewalk traffic and adult beverages while sounds of bowling balls against "duck" pins filled the air. By the mid-1970s, the same building housed various bars. Dale Bales's Dancing Bear (later the Windbreaker) still had the maple floors of the bowling lanes. Dale was a booking agent and had nationally known acts coming through the bar for a minimal cover charge. I remember Marshal Chapman walking out onto the stage with a fifth of Jack Daniels in one hand and a Heineken in the other, yelling, "Let's party!"

I clearly recall the first day that the effervescent Miss Darlena Goodwin walked down Center Street. She was so beautiful "you could almost hear the promises break."[1] Darlena, Gloria Kosko, Daryl Bonnette, and Suzzana (rosanadana) Scruggs opened a vegetarian sidewalk café and ran it from one of those hinged side openings of the

---

1   From the song "Trouble" by Todd Snider

old bowling alley in the summer of 1978. Hugh Merritt's A&M grocery at Center and West Ashley gave way to Monk's Corner run by Dean and Jeanean Monk, which added spice and a pre-Bert's atmosphere to Center Street.

Richard Weatherford and his sons maintained the Sand-Dollar Social Club, the best rock and roll beach bar within driving distance, as a private club ($1.00 per year). Loud, raucous, smoky, and full of the Folly's characters, the Sand-Dollar was the place where the Charleston's elite came to slum. The motorcycles out front stood silent sentinel as people too drunk to stand were leaned against one another like tottering tombstones in the front booth. The bar was welcoming to the locals but seemed just dangerous enough to keep the faint-hearted visitor from crossing the threshold.

In the late 1970s, Bushy's (now Marsh Winds condos) and the Sand Bar restaurant each had all-you-can-eat buffets for under $7 and were wonderful watering holes. Darus Weathers, owner of the Sandbar Restaurant, recently reminded me that a seafood platter was all of $2.50 in 1978. Bushy's restaurant (owned by Bushy Peak) had the wheelhouse of an old shrimp boat as part of the decor of the main dining area. (The rumor was that Bushy created his namesake restaurant with the proceeds of the sale of Sam's Red and White Grocery on Hwy. 17 South, which he had won from Sam Rhodes in a poker game.)

In May 1982, Larry Ridgeway spearheaded the first Folly festival and dubbed it "The Great Folly Beach Reunion," and it truly was. People

who loved Folly came to visit and walk down Center Street greeting old friends with beers and smiles. Silkworm screen printing provided the logo.

In 1985, Mr. McKevlin built a new surf shop and the old bowling alley was destroyed except for a small portion which went on to house Café Suzanne—where Lee and Suzanne Chewning provided the locals their equivalent of the TV show bar "Cheers" while serving gourmet presentations of local seafood.

The Dumbwaiter (formerly Andre's Seafood Restaurant) on the north side of the bridge had Vivian's she-crab soup, crab cakes, grouper cheeks, and the most idyllic atmosphere for dissolving into your surroundings that one could imagine. Mrs. Lottie Harvey and her family made sure you could always count on the Sanitary Restaurant for good food and strong coffee in mugs that were a good half-inch thick. The Seashell (now Snapper Jack's) offered breakfast and lunch and a damn fine old-fashioned cheeseburger cooked on a well-seasoned grill.

The Folly Beach Post Office, managed by Jimmy Ballard and Joy Stringer for many years, started out at Tom and Kitty Winges' Newsstand on Center Street. It then moved to the building that later housed Turtle Corner Grocery and then to the East Indian Avenue location with L.D. Suggs at the helm. During the 1970s and 1980s, Wes and Francis Murphy made Turtle Corner Grocery (now Follywood) a gathering point for the island with easy humor, the time to talk, and their fingers on the pulse of the community.

John Chrysostom's Sea Turtle Variety Store was on the corner of West Cooper and Center Street right where his son Paul runs it today. Next door, Steven's 5 and 10 Cent Store became Aieda's, which offered vintage clothing, a pharmacy, and antiques. Aieda's was the place to go for eccentric clothes and estate jewelry. Every purchase was served with a side of the hyperkinetic, mostly one-sided conversation that Aieda Johnson was known for. Folly Liquors became Mr. Bill's Bar in the building now occupied by the Crab Shack.

Atlanta native Doug David created Folly Beach Cable. We all lost sleep to VH-1 and MTV for a couple of months. A crowd of skateboarders routinely gathered in front of the storefront's TV and stood mesmerized by the opportunity of seeing their favorite artists in a music video.

Mike Slater and Suzanne Palmer brought Beach Paddle Tennis to Folly when they moved here from St Augustine, Florida in the early 1980s. A club formed that had 30 regular players. The club and its players were well respected and hosted regional and national tournaments on Folly. Courts were marked in the sand using Folly's long, flat, low tide beach. Pipes set in concrete filled tires served as the uprights for the nets.

Paddle tennis still life. *Larry Ridgeway's collection.*

The 1,200-square-foot two-story city hall was at street level. In the 1950s, the town's only fire engine occupied a bay in the same building. By the 1970s, the bay had been closed and turned into part of the police station—and the two American LaFrance fire engines occupied a separate building behind city hall. The police department had a jail with two cells that opened onto the alley behind the building. As you walked by, you could sometimes hear the occupants calling out for mercy. Almost on display, those two holding cells were tangible reminders of the cost of bad decisions.

AM radio was still king and the Mighty 690, WAPE (AHH-EEE-AHH) out of Jacksonville Florida, boasted 50,000 watts of AM power bouncing off the ionosphere all the way to Charleston. A local character, Wolfman, would do a perfect impression of syndicated DJ Wolfman Jack without even being asked. Our Wolfman could be seen daily, doing his fully-seated balancing act on the bench outside of the of the Sand-Dollar.

Roy and Nan Carter ran Carter's Barbershop and practiced their trade in the small space beside the Sea Turtle Variety Store for fifteen years before moving to the single-story brick building that used to occupy the southwest corner West Cooper and Center Street. Roy cut hair for another twenty years. The building also housed Shelton Realty, where Paul and Carolyn Shelton sat at their separate desks filling the room with conversations with their clients and friends. In the late 1980s, Gloria Bisman took over from the Carters and introduced us to both her loving nature and her huge collection of memorabilia honoring her hero, Mickey Mouse.

Folly had Thompson's Marina and Crosby's for fresh seafood. Carl Ott ran the boat yard at 9th Street West with a haul out for shrimp boats. In the 1980s, the boat yard gave way to the Clam Farm at which the first experimentation on clam mariculture in South Carolina was conducted by Dr. John Manzi and the rest of the eclectic and beer loving clam farmers.

Chris and Jerry Spetceris ran Chris and Jerry's Grocery in the building that Bert's Market now occupies. They always had fresh feta and big wooden casks of calamata olives and big dill pickles. There were homemade Greek specialties like dolmades and spanakopita, all served with an attitude. Pete's Hot Dogs on the beach in the 100 block of East Arctic

Carter's Barbershop, where Gloria Bisman presided.

had the best hot dog chili I have ever tasted. Smoak's and Shuster's Float Stands at East Second Street would rent you a blue and yellow rubberized canvas float by the hour or the day. In the late 1970s and early 1980s, the bars on the beach on the east side of the pier were the kind of bars in which it was probably best not to take a glass for your beer if offered one.

A postcard of the east end of seawall looking east from the early 1960s. *Photo by Boss Wilbanks in the Wilbanks collection.*

The Atlantic House offered South Carolina's only bar over the open surf, but the quality of the food was marginal at best. It's the only restaurant I ever refused to eat at, even if someone else was paying. Doris Snider's Village Tackle Shop on Center Street (the Washout) offered gasoline, fishing tackle, hot dogs, a pool table, beer, and sodas from a metal ice chest.

Surfing was popular on Folly, so not surprisingly, the town had shops to support this pastime. McKevlin's Surf Shop, the first surf shop on Folly and one of the first in this part of the country, was established in the rear of the bowling alley in 1965 with the irascible Dennis McKevlin at the helm. Dewey's Surf Shop, run by Dewey Mauldin, followed close behind. Dewey's later became the Natural Arts Surf Shop run by Ricky Koger. Bill Perry and Betty Sue Cowsert took over from Ricky and renamed the shop Oceansports Surf Shop, where Bill Perry and his friend Bill Bartlett coined the moniker that will forever identify Folly Beach as "The Edge of America." John Kalagian and his wife Susan Bogart opened Barrier Islands Surf Shop on Center Street after the International Motor Sports Association (IMSA) GT racing accident at Sebring, Florida that left John paralyzed and ended his driving career.

The population of Folly was so small and the locals were so well known that during the early 1980s, if you were a local and went down to Center Street...and had too much fun, it was police policy that you could get a ride home in a cruiser. We referred to this service as "Just Call."

Bird life was so plentiful that it was not uncommon to see fifty or sixty pelicans, flying in a large V-formation, gracing our morning and afternoon skies as Folly's "air force" flew back and forth between Lighthouse Inlet and their rookery on Bird Key.

I was living in paradise—a melting pot of unconventional personalities in a community so small and so accepting that people were both known and loved for their eccentricities. It was impossible to walk down Center Street without getting into a conversation with someone you knew. The businesses were locally owned and the owners made the bulk of their living on tourists in the summer—and either closed or were supported

The Folly Beach "Air Force"

by locals in the winter. Everyone knew everyone. No one got rich, but nobody starved, and everybody smiled.

Starting a dental practice has its stresses, but when I reached the causeway on my drive home and got my first glimpse of the wide horizon and the subtly changing seasonal palette of the spartina marsh shimmering in the low angle light of the afternoon sun, the cares of my day would melt away. I had the beach at my back door, a sailboat at the edge of the dunes, cold beer in the refrigerator, and a town full of good bars, music, and restaurants. And if all that wasn't enough, once a month I had the full moon to provide a path for me to take a night sail onto the ocean and back. It was a palpably unique and lovable place to live, and I had the most intense feeling of being at home I have ever experienced. Folly was the metaphysical center of the universe, the land of the walking wounded, and the epicenter of entropy—all rolled up into a cornucopia of plenty. It was heaven.

The images that follow will take you for a walk down Center Street in the mid-1980s. We start with a view of the old McKevlin's Bowling Alley at the ocean end of Center Street and move north down the east side of the street toward the bridge. When we get to Holland Realty, we will visually move back toward the ocean and end with a view toward the ocean end of Center Street before and after the construction of the Holiday Inn was begun.

McKevlin's Bowling Alley and Surf Shop looking east and south.

Sand-Dollar, Mac's "new" Surf Shop, and the Seashell—a view north down Center Street.

Florence and Boss Wilbanks' Folly Drug Sundries. In the 1970s, this was the location of the Seashell Restaurant, which is now Snapper Jack's.

A view south and east down Center Street from Cooper Street.

A view north of the east side of Center Street showing Sea Turtle Variety and adjacent businesses.

Folly Liquors, Aieda's Closet and Drug Store, and John's Tax Service.

Folly Liquors and Folly Court, the current home of Crab Shack.

Turtle Corner, the current home of Follywood, Beach Realty, and
steps that used to lead to Tommy and Kitty Weinges' Newsstand.

Fred Holland Realty.

A view south and east down Center Street from Huron Avenue.

Doris Snider's Village Tackle Shop, the current home of the Washout.

Folly Beach City Hall

Carter's Barbershop (later Gloria Bisman's) and Shelton Realty.

View north of the Sand-Dollar and A&M Market.

A view of the end of Center Street prior to the construction of the Holiday Inn.

A view down Center Street when the Holiday Inn was under construction.

The Atlantic House, which was destroyed during Hurricane Hugo.

Bushy's Restaurant, which had a shrimp boat wheelhouse in the dining area.
Today, Marsh Winds Condominiums are at this location.

Folly Island

Chapter 3

Folly's Origin Story

Folly's name is thought to have evolved from the Old English word *follie* used by early sailors to describe the heavily wooded islands along the coast. The island has also been referred to by two other names. Early maps refer to Folly Island as Coffin Land. It is assumed that it got this designation because of shipwrecks that involved sick passengers or that it was the most convenient place to disembark the sick, dead, and dying so ships could clear the quarantine station on Morris Island. But it was not uncommon for early maps to also assign the name of Coffin Land to Morris Island.

The ever-shifting shoals that guarded the entrance to Charleston harbor made navigation dangerous—both islands were equally likely to have experienced shipping disasters. Both islands were also likely places to see the burial of passengers that had succumbed to greatly feared diseases.

On a more positive note, Folly is also known as the "Sleeping Lady" for her distinct resemblance to a prone female figure with her head to the west and her feet to the east.

However, when the island was granted to proprietor William Rivers in 1696, it was legally known as Folly Island. Early maps and anecdotal evidence indicate there was an active plantation on Folly— and that it used slave labor until the Civil War. Folly was home to the Union invasion force of some 13,000 troops that laid siege to Charleston between November 1863 and February 1865.

The island changed hands many times before it was purchased by the Folly Island Company in 1918. With this purchase, the island began to be used for recreation. As there were no roads to the island, a small steamer, the *Ataquin*, transported people to Folly from the City Wharf at the west end of Tradd Street via the Stono River. The fare was $1.00 for adults, $.50 for children.

By the mid-1920s, rivers and creeks had been bridged to form a toll road that allowed automobile access to the island. The Citizens and Southern Company bought the island in 1925 and began Folly's development as a beach resort, bringing electric lights and an improved toll road that served the community until the South Carolina highway system took control of it in June of 1943.

Political Folly

Folly Island had no formal legal identity until it became a township in 1936. Its commissioners were appointed by the Charleston County Legislative Delegation and approved by the governor. The Legislative Delegation exerted a fair amount of control over the political and economic fortunes—Folly Township had some but not all the rights of a municipality. An attempt to incorporate the town in 1952-53 proved unsuccessful.

From township to city

Jack Wilbanks was the person most responsible for Folly's becoming a municipality (city). The Home Rule Act, which decentralized government and gave more power to local jurisdictions, did not pass until 1975. But it was being considered during the period that Jack was working toward Folly's incorporation and he was sure that becoming a city would guarantee the community the most independent status. He saw that incorporation would both clarify Folly's legal status and provide for improved financial self-determination.

Jack moved to Folly as a child with his family in 1942, grew up here, and served his hometown in some capacity for most of his life. A precocious child, he always seemed to do things unusual for his years. For example, as a teenager, he took an interest in fire and rescue and was actively involved in rescues you might expect would require a little more age. By age thirty-five, he had served as a fireman, the youngest ever Civic Club president, a township commissioner, and a township chairman. A progressive, Jack focused on community improvement grants and systems modernization. He was a voracious reader and a natural leader quick to take charge. His self-deprecating sense of humor allowed him to shoulder criticism without offense.

From the mid-1960s through the 1970s, Folly was a southern insular community—800 people in the winter—with few children. From Memorial Day to Labor Day, it became a tourist town and returned to its comfortable isolation the other seven months. About 50% of the property owners were part-time or absentee, and dilapidated houses were a major blight. Most people who lived on Folly full-time had either been there or owned property most of their lives. They had adopted an if-it-ain't-broke-don't-fix-it attitude toward progress.

Jack first created friction with local and absentee owners by securing grants in 1968 to clean up the dilapidated shacks that were a common sight on the beach. Unfortunately, the people who owned the shacks didn't want to maintain them. But they also didn't want the uppity kid they had seen grow up on the island telling them what to do.

In the mid-1960s, as township chairman, Jack made contact with the South Carolina Municipal Association and got other members of the township government to go to their meetings. He was convinced that the only way Folly would reach its full potential was to incorporate and become a city, and despite the obstacle of inertia, he assembled the necessary support to move forward with an attempt to incorporate the island. Henry Flood acted as chairman of the Folly Beach Incorporation Committee.

The concept of incorporation was not universally embraced—some people in the community and on the town council were adamantly opposed. They were concerned about several issues.

Their fear was that being incorporated and fully responsible for all aspects of governing would be too expensive and complicated. They also resented the plan because it proposed that the incorporation would be done piecemeal rather than including all the town at once— an approach that limited voter participation. Some wanted to remain a township because, as such, Folly could not qualify for a grant to fund sewer service.

As Herbert Alexander, spokesman for the anti-incorporation group, said, "Incorporation is a part of a plan to bring in outside commercial interests and change the character of the island." This particular concern became the galvanizing fear that drove the controversies about development on Folly in the 1980s.

One other reason that incorporation was a contested issue was that some just didn't like Jack Wilbanks's governing style, nor did they trust his assessment of the benefits versus the costs of changing from a township to a city.

As a result, a tug of war ensued between those who favored remaining a township and those who favored incorporation.

South Carolina law required that the electors (voters) own 50% of the assessed value of the area seeking to be incorporated. Unfortunately, the voting members of the island only owned 48% of the total value of the property, with the other 52% owned by absentee and non-voting members of the community.

Through gerrymandering, those who were interested in incorporation carved out the geography, value, and votes required by dividing Folly into four areas and addressing them one at a time. Jack and Henry and a committee of 22 citizens worked hard to make this all come together, a complicated endeavor that involved driving to different parts of the state to convince absentee owners to become voters and support incorporation.

The property incorporated first, in 1972, was not even contiguous with the island proper—it was Long Island, which is north of Folly between the mainland and Oak Island (see map on facing page).

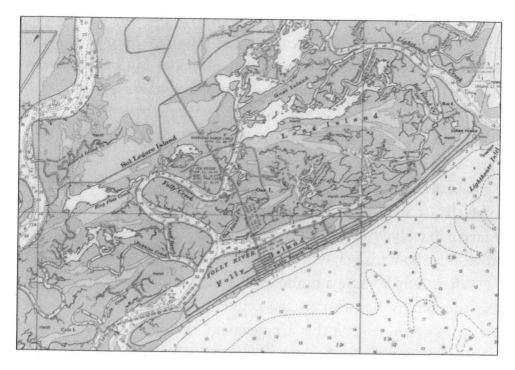

So, for a period, there was both a township and a city operating within the boundaries of Folly Island, with the township maintaining the commanding role in governance. Marlene Estridge (now celebrating over forty years of service to Folly) remembers keeping two sets of books.

Having two governments on the same island created logistical and financial burdens that eventually fell most heavily on the township. Gerald Davis, one of the township commissioners at the time, told me that in 1973, the township commissioners, led by Dennis McKevlin, begrudgingly voted to disband and fold all of Folly into the incorporation effort.

On August 1, 1973, then-South Carolina Secretary of State O. Frank Thornton granted permission to hold the final incorporation referendum. The election itself was held on September 5. The result: 173 for, 85 opposed. All the parts of Folly were now united and the City of Folly Beach was born.

Peace like a river, right? Unfortunately not. The personality clashes and summative grievances that had accumulated during the transition from township to municipality had created hard feelings that lingered.

A lawsuit challenging the validity of the election was filed immediately by the opponents of the incorporation—Herbert Alexander, Helen Barbrey, Harry Beckman, and Merle Rounsaville—but the Charleston County District Court ruled that the incorporation was legal.

Johnny Douglas was elected as Folly's first mayor and Fred Adams, Jack Wilbanks, Marvin Estridge, Ed Smoak, and Ed Wilder comprised the first city council. Jack Wilbanks and Marvin Estridge prevailed upon local artist Jim Booth to design the city seal.

When Folly became a municipality, the community had chosen the council-manager (strong manager) form of government. In this arrangement, the mayor is a figurehead who has no greater legal power than a councilperson. The mayor and council create policy and the city manager is a professional employee with the legal power and responsibility to both implement that policy and manage the employees.

The decision to have a strong manager/weak mayor form of government was largely due to Jack, who believed (somewhat naively for Folly) that the community would be best served by a government in which the professional management of the city would be separated from politics.

The City Council interviewed two candidates for the manager's position and decided it didn't want either of them. Jack was interested, so the council chose him to become the first city manager of Folly Beach.

As city manager, Jack became a paid employee. The strong manager form of government gave him considerable power that he never missed an opportunity to exercise. Unfortunately, Jack was headstrong and unwilling to compromise when there were differences of opinion. He was seen as a my-way-or-the-highway kind of manager.

Jack said, "Sure, I make enemies quickly. I make friends quickly, too. Anytime you are active and publicly state your opinion, there's a tendency to become a polarizing person."

He was right, but in spades. His outspokenness and strong-willed use of power gradually divided the community into two camps. He was loved by many as a straight-talking public servant who was modernizing the community's systems and successfully bringing in grant money for city improvements. Those people were grateful for his intelligence and talents and appreciated his pugnacious progressivism. But others found him abrasive, aggressive, and inflexible. In a word—intolerable. His aggressive promotion of laws that restricted surfing added to the cloud of controversy that already surrounded him.

In return for agreeing to incorporate, the voters had been promised that the entire City Council would stand for reelection within three months. Charleston's morning paper, the *News and Courier*, stated, "Folly's politics could be called a lot of things, but apathetic would never be one of them."

The divisions over how the new city would be run and by whom arrived fully dressed at that second municipal-wide election in March 1974. Sides had already been chosen. There were three candidates for mayor and fifteen candidates for the six council seats. The leading candidates for mayor—Johnny Douglas and Fred Adams—both ran with a slate of council candidates.

Incumbent mayor Johnny Douglas and Jack Wilbanks were close.

Challenger Fred Adams and Dennis McKevlin were close.

Their two opposing camps were not.

Fred and his slate won the election and the friction between Jack Wilbanks and the duo of Fred Adams and Dennis McKevlin and their supporters began in earnest. This tension would be exacerbated by legal conflicts...with the surfing community.

Chapter 4

Eastern Surfing Association v. City of Folly Beach

An uneasy relationship between the township of Folly and the surfing community had existed since 1966, when the township passed the first ordinance limiting where and when surfing was legal. Then, in 1972, when Folly was in transition between township and city, the fledgling government escalated the conflict with the surfing community by further limiting surfing. The conflict between Folly and the surfers would turn out to be a catalyst for big changes on Folly.

At the time, the Eastern Surfing Association had not yet penetrated the island. Two surfing clubs had formed on Folly—the Palmetto Surf Club and the Tri-Island Surfing Society, but not all surfers belonged.

The bad behavior of the outliers created enough ill will between the citizens and the surfing community that surfers were generally seen as a menace. Frequent episodes of surfers trespassing and damaging property did not help their reputation. There was also bad blood between surfers and the pier fishermen, who would aim their casts at the surfers to dissuade them from "ruining" their fishing. And, to make matters worse, loose surfboards would sometimes hit swimmers in the surf.

The distrust and antagonism between surfers and the citizenry got so bad that the township tried to further limit surfing. Jack Wilbanks formulated the changes and the then township amended the 1966 law in September 1972, creating even more restrictions on where and when surfing was permitted.

Dennis McKevlin promptly accused commissioner Johnny Douglas of being anti-surfer, saying he had "accomplished as a commissioner what he could not as a citizen" by creating restrictions that kept surfers away from the front of his house.

The change in the surfing laws further distanced Jack Wilbanks and Johnny Douglas from McKevlin, who got elected to City Council and became the surfing community's advocate.

The main issue between the surfing community and the township was that the parts of the beach surfers were restricted to didn't have the best surf. That was a problem—and it became a bigger problem one late September afternoon after the new restrictions had been put in place.

Sometimes the hurricanes that pass offshore of the Edge of America in the fall will leave in their wake days too beautiful to fully comprehend. The storms create big swells as they pass and then take the energy out of the atmosphere as they move up the coast. Once past, the storminess melts away, leaving balmy days with a 15-mile horizon, Simpson clouds, and well-formed waves that make for wonderful surfing.

It was on just such a day that Ricky Koger, Lindy Corely, Howie Davis, Michael Urrichio, and Bill Hood stood side by side and stared in united disappointment at the poor quality of the waves in the section they were restricted to. All were local boys—this was their beach. And with the devil-may-care attitude typical of twenty-year-old males, they looked at each other and said, "Screw it! Let's go surfing."

The best surfing was in the 2100 block of East Ashley Avenue because the sandbars that migrated on shore from Lighthouse Inlet produced a predictable shore break. It was also the quietest part of the beach. There were few homes—and those were mostly empty since the summer had passed. The boys thought there was a good chance they could surf where they weren't allowed and not be noticed. They got into three cars and rode down to the east end of the beach.

The swells that day were chest high with an offshore breeze to stand them up and help them keep their form longer. The five young men had a ball as they rode wave after wave. Then, late in the afternoon, they regrouped and sat on their boards outside of the surf line to talk about their rides. It was then that they noticed a small crowd gathering on the beach—and the red lights of the town's only police cruiser. A disgruntled homeowner had reported them and the authorities were assembled to bring them to justice.

Chief Fred Jenowski, "Ski," got on the bullhorn and said, "You boys are in violation of our surfing ordinance. I want you to come in to shore right now." The boys didn't move.

The chief repeated his demand several times. The five young men looked at each other and said, "You know what? We don't get conditions like this every day and since no one can actually get to us out here in the ocean, let's just surf and deal with the consequences later." They ignored the chief and paddled into position for their next rides.

The next time they stopped to rest, they reassembled before the persistent crowd on the beach and noticed someone paddling out to them. It was Rex Whitcomb.

This was a problematic moment for Rex. He was not only a peer, friend, and fellow surfer, but also a police officer. A native of Folly who had been involved in police and fire actions since he was a teenager, Rex didn't like the surfing restrictions himself. He resolved most confrontations over surfing outside the permitted places by calling the offenders in from the surf and redirecting them to the designated areas. Rex knew these young men well and approached the surfers, with an uneventful return to the shore as his imagined outcome.

Rex glided up to Ricky. "You guys have got to come in."

Ricky shook his head. "I hear what you're sayin' Rex, but this is all bull. We are not hurting a soul. There's nobody on the beach but us, so I think we're just gonna stay out here and surf."

"I know. I think the law is stupid too, but everybody's upset. I hate it, but I'm asking you to come with me so, come on now, let's go."

As Rex finished his sentence, he grabbed the nose of Ricky's board. When he did, Ricky grabbed his board and flipped him off it. With Rex's hope of a peaceful resolution dashed, the quintet of newly minted "criminals" went back to surfing.

It wasn't dusk, but it was getting there and soon, it was too dark for the boys to surf safely. The crowd on the beach had thinned and the young men thought about how they could get back to the shore—and their cars—without getting caught.

Bill Hood paddled west to sneak back to his car, but he was apprehended and detained. Meanwhile, Ricky, Michael, Lindy, and Howie made a break for Mike Holmes's beach house nearby. Mike was a friend and they hoped his daddy, Connie, would be home. Connie ran Charleston Wrecking Company and was well-known and well-connected in Charleston and elsewhere.

The quartet made it to their destination without being caught. Howie and Lindy successfully eluded the police and got back to Howie's car. Connie *was* home, saw it all unfold, and brought Ricky and Michael upstairs where they would be safe and warm. Michael Urrichio called *his* father, Paul, a prominent attorney known in legal circles as the "Pope of Broad Street." No one who knew anything about Charleston would take either Connie or Paul lightly.

When the red lights showed up in front of Connie's house, he walked down the driveway to intercept the chief.

"Good evening, Connie, how are you?" said the chief.

Connie nodded. "I'm just fine, thank you, Ski. I hope you are. What can I do for you?"

"I know you got those boys who were surfing illegally in your house. I'm asking you to turn them over to me. They've got a lot of people upset."

"I'd love to help you, but first I've got a question for you."

"Shoot."

"Have you got a warrant?"

The chief narrowed his eyes. "No, I don't have a warrant. I'm just trying to do my job. Can't you and the four of them just cooperate so we can wrap this up?"

Connie looked squarely at the chief. "As I said, Ski, I'd love to help you, but without a warrant, I'm afraid that I can't. These boys were just surfing on a beautiful afternoon off a deserted beach, for Christ's sake. Why can't you just leave them alone and let everybody learn a lesson without this going any further?"

"I can't do that."

"Then I guess we're finished here. I hope you have a pleasant evening." Connie turned and walked back to the house.

Shortly afterward, Michael's father arrived, and he had a plan. "Ricky," he said. "I want you two to get in your car and follow me off the beach. If we get stopped, let me do the talking."

Between the time Paul Urrichio showed up and the two-car caravan left the Holmes's house, the police chief and several citizens had set up a road block at the washout, preventing passage from the east end of the island. As the two cars approached the roadblock, the chief signaled for Paul to stop.

"What's this all about?" said Paul.

The chief nodded to Paul. "We're trying to catch some surfers who were surfing illegally today."

Paul said, "I know, I was talking to Connie about it."

The chief glanced at someone standing by Ricky's car. "Are those boys the ones that were surfing?" he yelled.

"I really can't say for sure," responded the person. I only recognize the one that's driving, and he's definitely one of the surfers."

So it was that Michael escaped identification but Ricky Koger joined Bill Hood, who had been arrested earlier. They were the only two to face charges that night. When they reached the station, Ricky called his parents and learned that his father was in the hospital. Someone had recognized Ricky's car and had called the Kogers to let them know that he was in a lot of trouble and would be arrested. Ricky's dad was so distressed that he experienced chest pain and had to be taken to the emergency room.

When Ricky heard about his father, he got pretty upset. Paul stepped in to try to settle Ricky down and informed the police that he would be representing Ricky and Bill if they were charged. Thanks to the chaos surrounding Ricky's father and the respect the chief had for Paul, neither Ricky nor Bill was charged that night.

However, this incident was the catalyst for two lawsuits brought in state court over the next three years that were aimed at reinstating surfers' rights to unrestricted surfing. Both alleged a loss of the surfers' constitutional rights and both were dismissed without going to trial.

Revival and victory

Ben Peeples moved to Folly Beach, fresh out of law school, in 1974. A surfer himself, he was irritated by the fact that he couldn't just walk out of his front door and go surfing—and saw the regulations as a violation of his rights. As he got to know other surfers, he learned about the two previous attempts to overturn the surfing laws and studied the cases. Having the advantage of knowing what *not* to do, he planned and executed a third lawsuit.

The 1964 Civil Rights Act and the Equal Protection Clause of the U.S. Constitution's 14th Amendment indicate that in the case of any conspiracy that deprives an individual or a group of their constitutional rights, the aggrieved may file for relief in federal court. So, instead of filing in state court, Ben took the initiative to sue in federal court and included a $50,000 damage claim. Because Ben filed the suit, he couldn't be the plaintiff, so the Eastern Surfing Association agreed to be named in the suit and helped by providing two plaintiffs and some funding.

As soon as the suit was filed, more money began to come in. One day a check appeared in his mailbox for $2,000 from Clark Foam Company. (Clark made the foam blanks that individual board manufacturers used to create custom surfboards.) This money was enough for Ben to hire the director of beaches from Huntington, California as an expert witness. He could also afford to appeal if the verdict went against him.

Other people soon got involved. Bill Perry and Betty Sue Cowsert of Oceansports Surf Shop helped the local surfers form the Charleston Surfing Association. The local surfers raised money and chipped in with manpower to document conditions on the busiest weekends to help refute the city's claims that surfers posed a danger to the public.

The case went to court with Carl Earl Simons Jr. as the presiding judge and Bobby Hood as attorney for the city.

When the suit was filed, Judge Simons asked for briefs from both sides, as is customary. If a judge feels the law clearly favors one party to the suit, he or she might counsel the plaintiff and defendant before the trial is slated to begin.

Two days before the jury trial was to start, Judge Simons asked Mr. Peeples and Mr. Hood to join him in his chambers. The judge told Mr. Hood that the law was not on the city's side, that the city was likely to lose, and that if the surfers succeeded, he would recommend to the jury that a cash settlement of $50,000 be awarded to the plaintiffs. In short, he suggested that the city settle the case.

At first, Hood demurred. Until, that is, Judge Simons reminded him that while state statutes might provide sovereign immunity protection for city council members for harm done to individuals or groups, there was no immunity for public officials from group and individual responsibility for damage done in violation of a plaintiff's broader constitutional rights. When Judge Simons asked Hood to go back to the City Council and ask the most financially secure member how he felt about being personally responsible for a part of the settlement, the city attorney saw the light. One day later, the city agreed to let Peeples write the new surfing law.

The ordinance that passed City Council eliminated most restrictions and greatly expanded the area available for surfing. In the spirit of cooperation, Peeples included one of the first laws in the country requiring that surfboards be attached to the surfer with a leash.

After the lawsuit was settled in 1976, the city asked Ben Peeples to be its city attorney. He would serve in that capacity for 40 years and one day.

Chapter 5

A Change Is Gonna Come

The outcome of the conflict with the surfing community and Mayor Douglas's and Jack Wilbanks's role in the dispute made some on City Council wonder whether this "strong manager" form of government was the best choice. Dennis McKevlin and the younger members of the community had become more energized against Jack during the three years that the surfing lawsuits were in play.

Mayor Fred Adams and Councilman Dennis McKevlin gathered enough signatures to petition the Secretary of State for an election to decide whether to keep the strong manager form of government (adopted at incorporation) or change to a strong mayor form, which would give the bulk of the power to the mayor and council and reduce the role of city manager to a more subordinate position.

Johnny Douglas & Jack Wilbanks
Strong Manager Proponents

Fred Adams & Dennis McKevlin
Strong Mayor Proponents

The tension between Jack and his opponents had reached the point that something had to give. Jack was already setting his sights on advancing in his career and was about to complete his master's degree in city administration. Well aware of the politics in play—and the jeopardy he was in—he worried about his job security and his family's welfare.

In short, Jack had become a flash point. If the community changed its governance structure as Fred and Dennis hoped, Jack would likely be removed from Folly's government altogether. Jack's widow tells me that he knew it was time to go, but he was a true believer in the advantages of the strong manager arrangement as the form that minimized political interference in the day-to-day operation of the city. He wanted that form of government to prevail even if he would not be able to remain a part of it and tried to keep from being the focus of the election.

After almost four years in his position as city manager, Jack resigned on January 21, 1976, effective at the end of May. On March 16, the community voted to make the change from strong manager to strong mayor and shortly afterward, in a separate election, chose Fred Adams as mayor of the government (reconfigured for the second time in two years). Fred's first official act was to fire and replace the entire business staff of the city.

Jack left Folly Beach in 1976 and went on to have a successful career and a long tenure as the town manager of Summerville under Mayor Berlin G. Meyers. But Fred's tenure as mayor of the reconfigured government was a short one. I was told by both Fred Adams and his wife Bobby that Bobby's health problems were not helped by the lingering discord over the change in the form of government and the fact that Fred had fired the entire city staff right after he got elected. Fred's term as mayor proved so difficult for him and his wife that shortly after the election, he announced his desire to resign.

Fred was a popular mayor, and the City Council offered him a leave of absence to give him and Bobby time to work through their problems, but it wasn't meant to be. Fred resigned by letter in December 1976, just nine months after he had been elected. In a special election, Regas Kennedy was selected to serve out Fred's unexpired term, which would end in 1978—just as my own adventure was about to begin.

Chapter 6

A Toe in the Water

When Fred Adams approached me in my office about running for City Council in 1977, politics was the farthest thing from my mind. Although I had held positions of responsibility in college and dental school, I was not a political person. I was 32 years old and was so apolitical that I had never even registered to vote.

But the more I thought about running, the more appealing the idea became. I wanted to help preserve the quality of life I enjoyed and be a part of finding a solution to the erosion problem at Folly. I wrote a letter asking for support, knocked on countless doors, and met a score of Folly's characters. That same year, Regas Kennedy ran for a full term as mayor against Gerald Davis and C.M. Phillips and won handily.

Twelve people ran for three council seats. I was elected and, in my first two years as a councilman, served with Mayor Kennedy and councilmen Francis Wilborn, Lavern James, Dennis McKevlin, Don Singletary Jr., and Bert Ketcham.

After I was elected, I soon realized that getting involved was not for the faint of heart. I was unaware of the earlier political history, but I would soon learn for myself that on Folly, politics is a blood sport, and getting elected to its government might have been the quickest way for me to get past an unrealistic expectation that everybody would like me.

My first term began on May 9, 1978 with my first City Council meeting. At that meeting, Bill Lee, the chairman of the community's first erosion committee, gave their final report. This committee had been formed a year earlier, made up of Bill Lee, D.C. Liollio, C.W. Benson Sr.,

John D. Ohlandt, Jack Devlin, Dr. Steven Bartlett, and Millard Hodge. Their conclusion was that the Charleston Harbor Navigation Project (CHNP), completed in 1895, was the root cause of Folly's erosion problems.

Before that meeting, the committee and the City Council had tried unsuccessfully to come to agreement with the U.S. Army Corps of Engineers' Charleston District Office on the role of the jetties in Folly's beach erosion. Having failed to make any progress, City Council sued the Corps for reparations.

I asked several questions at the meeting and before the night was over, I was the chairman of a new erosion committee, charged with continuing the city's efforts to find a solution to its erosion problems.

My first task was to become familiar with coastal processes. So I went to the Florida Shore and Beach Preservation Association's annual meeting in December 1978 and began my education.

Chapter 7

National Attention, Local Chaos

As a result of the work of the first erosion committee, the 1979 state legislature raised its annual appropriation for managing the state's beach front problems from $150,000 to $600,000—$440,000 of which was earmarked for Folly to fund a thus-far undefined solution to its erosion problem.

After my election, Dr. John Manzi, a local marine scientist, and Dr. Margaret Davidson, the second head of the South Carolina Sea Grant Consortium, secured a National Science Foundation grant and funded a multidisciplinary "Workshop on Erosion Abatement" to help Folly and the state decide the best use of those funds. The conference was held December 13–14, 1979, at Fort Johnson Marine Lab.

One conclusion at the workshop was that Folly needed a "renourishment" program and, until that was established, most of the $440,000 from the state should be banked. However, our state representative, Paul Gelegotis, informed us that holding the money in trust was not an option.

As per the recommendations of the workshop, the erosion committee asked and received permission from the state to spend the money on repairing several groins, rebuilding the dune line by beach scraping, and improving public access through the construction of walkovers at as many of our 57 platted public access ways as possible.

I asked my friend and local architect Dinos Liollio, whose family had a long history on Folly, to design a walkover that could be adopted as a prototype walkover for the state. He agreed and included a design for the first wheelchair accessible ramps at West 9th Street and East 16th Street. The erosion committee wanted ours to be a model project that would involve competitive bidding and gain state recognition as a first-rate effort, so I presented our concept to Mayor Kennedy.

He had a different take. He was sure that the city could get a group of local volunteers to build the walkovers in their spare time and, in doing so, save money and increase the number of walkovers.

The erosion committee was adamant that this project be an unassailable example of the wise use of state funding. None of us was ready to accept less than a by-the-book approach, but the mayor would not budge. He and I got into a heated disagreement over how the project would be done. The meeting ended with me shouting and Mayor Kennedy threatening to resign.

The disagreement over how the walkovers would be built was not the only issue at play. The relationship between the administration and council had become contentious. There were issues with the police department's handling of its affairs and questions about the efficiency of the Public Works Department, building inspection, and faith in the city's administration. Shortly after my argument with the mayor and a City Council meeting full of people that were very angry that Mayor Kennedy was so upset, Regas followed through on his threat. Almost everyone associated with the running of the city resigned as well.

Bam! Clerks, city administrator, the police and fire chief, officers, firemen, building inspector, the judge, the public works director all walked away. Lavern James, who was serving as mayor pro tempore, took over the the mayoral position.

Much of the community and most of City Council saw the argument over the walkovers and the subsequent resignation of the entire community administrative machinery as an outrage—and largely blamed me. Those who wanted change saw the leadership vacuum as an opportunity for improvement and got busy reassembling our city.

With the resignation of Chief Benson and the entire police and fire departments, the community was left with no police or fire protection. Thankfully, George Tittle Jr. stepped in as chief and did a great job implementing a public safety concept in which our officers would act as both policemen and firemen.

Folly's Police and Fire Department in 1980. Front row: John Manzi, Chief George Tittle, Gene Hollowell, and Paul Tittle; back row: Cliff Harvey, Brian Porter, me, Fred Bothman Jr., Tom Marshall, John Branks, Bob Stoertz, Ronnie Teal, and Paul Vansteenburgen (not pictured).

Chief Tittle worked out a mutual aid pact for fire protection with the James Island Public Service District, but we still had to have professionally trained staff available on the island. During the uncertainty that surrounded this transition period, Cliff Harvey and Brian Porter—local residents serving as volunteer firemen—were unmatched for their dedication. As the rebuilding of the department got underway, Bob Stoertz, John Manzi, Paul Vansteenburgen, and I joined the newly hired public safety officers and we all went through the state fireman certification course, with Les Colna (the king of malaprops) of the James Island Fire Department as our instructor. Most of us gracefully bowed out as new staff members were hired and trained, but Bob Stoertz served as a volunteer for years afterward.

One of the most important steps we took was to rehire Marlene Estridge to manage the office. It took some coaxing by Mayor James and Councilman Gerald Davis, but Marlene graciously agreed to get back into the city administration even though there was still a bad taste lingering from her dismissal when Mayor Fred Adams cleaned house after his election. With Marlene's help secured, we looked for a new city administrator. (At this writing, Marlene is still serving the city. She is Folly's touchstone.)

We hired Mr. William E. Griffin, who had a degree in public administration from Rutgers. With Bill hired, we modernized the city's administration, hiring Folly's first paid building inspector Ed (Lightning) Hull and a new public works director, Steve Robinson. We all relied on Larry Ridgeway, a successful business owner and recently elected councilman, to help Bill in evaluating and overseeing the modernization of the city's accounting systems.

Because we felt that Bill was overqualified, we asked him to give us at least a year of his service and presented him with a list of 17 tasks that needed to be done to bring the city up to speed. Bill accomplished those things in the first six months, including the first computerization of our books. Bill and Steve set out to replace all the broken water meters (we were billing for 30% less water than we were buying) and began to accurately account for our sale of water. Aside from property taxes, issuing traffic tickets and selling water were the city's two main profit centers. Bill Griffin served the city for more than ten years, somehow remaining above the pettiness of day-to-day politics on Folly through an especially contentious period.

Tearing down and then rebuilding the city did not endear my friend and new Councilman Larry Ridgeway and me to a good portion of the electorate. That period was the beginning of my alienation from the old guard politicians and it got tougher for me on the council. Politics became personal and binary.

The walkover project was competitively bid. We pushed up sand to create a protective dune line, repair 14 groins, and build 20 prototype walkovers, including the first two walkovers with handicapped access in the state. As of 2023, all are still functioning.

By 1980, I had become committed to working with several members of the community on quality-of-life issues and was uneasy about council's support of the erosion committee. I knew that I would need to become the mayor to be most effective at fulfilling my goals on both of those fronts. So I ran for mayor against acting Mayor Lavern James and our recently-resigned Police Chief Wallace Benson.

I came in second. Lavern would serve out the unexpired term of Mayor Kennedy, which would end in 1982. It was a good thing that Lavern was a calm, patient, and effective leader, because things were about to get very busy on Folly.

Chapter 8

How the Western Tip of Folly Island Became a County Park

On October 20, 1972, town dignitaries and developers met at the Sandbar Restaurant to unveil an ambitious $30 million proposal to develop most of the western tip of Folly. The development was to be named Bird Key. The plan included "some 910 dwellings, a yacht marina, a clubhouse and several landscaped parks." Given that the plan required the destruction of large areas of marsh, environmental concerns kept it from getting off the ground.

In 1977, following the failure of Bird Key, the South Carolina Parks, Recreation and Tourism Commission (SCPRT) approached Folly about building a state park there. City Council held a non-binding referendum seeking community input. The park concept was rejected on August 16 by a vote of 266 to 82. City Council said no thanks.

The First Rumble of Thunder from the Development Storm

Before I moved to Folly in 1975, there had been several failed attempts to develop condominium projects. At the time the major focus of the community was not on development but on beach erosion—the community had settled into the rhythms of the relative isolation brought on by worsening erosion problems and sagging real estate values. By 1980, things had changed and questions about growth moved to the front burner. As various development proposals appeared, the Council grew to be divided into two competing visions of Folly's future. Given that the City Council was only three years out from passing the 1977 Comprehensive Land-Use Plan Update, the members who had been part of its adoption believed that any growth that fit the plan should be allowed. By 1980, a growing number of citizens had come to believe that the 1977 plan was too pro-growth and that the community should be leveraging its inherent desirability into a future that favored conservative building heights and lowering the densities allowed by the plan.

Most of the community was not politically active and had not yet woken from the dream of living in paradise without having to defend it.

Early in 1979, Mariner's Cay Development Corporation bought Rook Island, a sparsely developed property across the Folly River on the west side of Folly Road. The island had a seafood processing shed run by Charlie Peyton, a shrimp boat dock, and a couple of residences. The developer got permission to tie into the sewer system run by the James Island Public Service District and ran a line to the island so they could build what is now Mariner's Cay Racquet and Yacht Club.

At the time that Mariner's Cay ran their sewer line, the property was not part of Folly Beach, but they soon asked to have it annexed. Mariner's Cay put sewer availability at the north foot of the Folly River bridge.

In late 1979, the western tip of Folly was in the news again. Columbia Management Corp. proposed a project called Sea Cabins for some of the same property as the failed Bird Key project. The proposal was to construct a tennis center and 540 prefabricated condominiums, which some of us called "Stack a Shacks"—our tongue-in-cheek name for the individually prefabricated mobile homes that were completely furnished, right down to the silverware. The modules were to be plugged into a preconstructed grid framework set on a piling foundation. Provision of sewer and water were required by our subdivision ordinance.

The developer advertised that the beach in front of the development would be private. As of 1977, the Coastal Zone Management Act posited that the state held all the lands below mean high water in public trust, so the proposal would probably have been found to be illegal, but it was never tested.

The majority of City Council thought the development was a great idea and was willing to allow the developer to run an exclusive sewer line from the west end of Folly to the Mariner's Cay sewer terminus to make the project a reality. Dennis McKevlin and I were the only two councilmen to vote against the project.

At the time, the property was a beautiful open dune field where it was not uncommon to find nude sunbathers, blanketed lovers seeking sanctuary, and overnight camping. Folly even got a nod from *Maxim* magazine naming the area one of the nation's better nude gay beaches.

Stories about the west end abounded. One of my favorites was one Officer Fred Bothman Jr. told me about, when he was called to the west end to address a complaint of a woman in the surf without a top on. Fred located the partially nude bather and motioned her out of the water. She slowly walked up close to him and said, "Yes?"

Fred said, "Ma'am, I am afraid that I am going to have to write you a ticket for indecent exposure."

She thought a minute, moved a little closer, and said, "You've seen my breasts, officer. Do you think they are indecent?"

Fred stammered a little, but said, "No ma'am, but they are illegal."

By 1980, the erosion problem at Folly had made Folly Beach Charleston County's least popular beach. Even though Edisto is more than ninety minutes away from Charleston, Folly was ranked behind Edisto in desirability by a News and Courier poll. Thanks to the erosion problem, City Council and many owners were understandably worried about what the future would bring and were desperately seeking any encouraging news. A fair number of people looked at Sea Cabins as a small bit of light in what must have seemed to be a long and dark tunnel. That perspective was understandable. The oceanfront, which had been the lifeblood of the community, was not a pretty sight.

The beach scenes that follow from the early 1980s show the condition of the beach and the vulnerability of many homes along Folly's shore.

West 5th Street looking east

East 8th Street looking east

East 15th Street looking west

East 2nd Street looking east

West 7th Street looking west

West 6th Street looking east

The property that the developer planned to use for its project had been purchased with financing from First Citizens Bank. Anticipating a clear path to construction, they applied for the necessary permits. Although the community was divided over whether the project was a good idea, there wasn't much vocal resistance, partly because projects like this had been proposed multiple times before and had not materialized.

In preparation for construction and sales, the development company moved a model unit the length of West Ashley Avenue to the site—the first time that something had been placed on the end of West Ashley that wasn't stick-built. The movers had to slash a lot of low hanging limbs from the particularly beautiful oak trees on West Ashley to put the unit in place. I got a call from Rogers Oglesby at 705 West Ashley. He was very upset over the damage they had done. Rogers, his wife Rita, and I sat together on his porch, had a vodka, and wept over the fact that this could happen in our quiet little community. We had come to believe that Folly was somehow immune to the perniciousness of high-density growth.

Shortly after that evening, John Manzi, Rogers Oglesby, Larry Ridgeway, and I formed a team and joined with several other residents to try to keep this development from happening.

The chess match begins

While we weren't happy that Sea Cabins was physically unappealing, structurally suspect, and out of scale with the existing character of our community, our main objection was rooted in the instability of the building site. The ends of barrier islands are notoriously unstable and unpredictable because the interplay of inlet currents and wave dynamics can change the position of the shoreline quickly. Time had proven (and has continued to prove) that the western tip of Folly Island is a dynamic piece of real estate.

The first coastal zone management law (Act 123) was enacted in 1977, so state management of the coastal zone was only four years old. Coastal zone management was administered by a brand new, semi-autonomous, quasi-legislative body called Coastal Council, under the direction of Dr.

Wayne Beam and State Senator James Waddell of Beaufort. Our questions regarding the unstable nature of the site were being raised eight years before the Beachfront Management Act of 1988.

In 1980, the only limits on development were based on the presence or absence of particular types of vegetation. Those limits did not affect the implementation of this development proposal. Coastal Council thought the project was a bad idea and didn't want it built, but they had no effective way of opposing it. The comprehensive zoning plan in effect at the time was passed in 1977 and this property was zoned Planned Residential Development (PRD), which allowed a wide variety of uses and population densities.

Larry Ridgeway was elected to council in 1980. Both Larry Ridgeway and I were new to City Council and the questions we raised about the appropriateness of this development fell on the deaf ears of the more senior majority of council. The Planning and Zoning Commission (P&Z) approved the project's preliminary plat.

With the majority of City Council squarely behind the idea, Larry, Rogers, John, and I weren't sure how we were going to successfully oppose it. We finally decided that, for want of a better tactic, we would to try to delay the P&Z's final approval. We felt that any day of delay was a day when there was still hope of finding way to keep Sea Cabins from happening.

P&Z's chairman was Bill Lee. We appealed to Bill in hopes of somehow slowing down the pace of the development's approval. He supported us and offered to hold bi-weekly environmental impact meetings so the community could learn about and comment on the project before the board granted its final approval. Larry, Rogers, John, and I raised public awareness and assembled scientific evidence against high-density construction on unstable sandspits.

South Carolina's shoreline management was rarely a consideration in development questions in the early 1980s, and there weren't many local resources to call on for information on best practices in coastal development. Dr. Margaret Davidson at the Sea Grant Consortium and Dr. Wayne Beam of Coastal Council were helpful in providing scientific support for our concerns. There was not enough time for us to generate much community concern.

The attitude of the majority of City Council was that any development on Folly was better than the depression that the community was experiencing. Most of City Council just couldn't imagine environmental concerns having a serious role to play in the appropriateness of a development.

The hearings began, held in a little room on the second floor of the old city hall. Typically, the "gang of four"—Larry, Rogers, John, and I—were joined by the developers and a small group of citizens—mostly business people—who saw the project as critical to Folly's rebirth. Thanks to Bill Lee's dedication, we held the developer off for six weeks. At the third meeting, an unexpected guest arrived with the developers—Morris Rosen, a prominent attorney. Morris listened patiently to our presentation and when it was over, he politely raised his hand to be recognized.

"Thank you for allowing me to speak," he said after introducing himself. "One of the greatest things about our country is the right of concerned citizens to participate in the decision-making processes of a community. I am particularly grateful for the people who have taken their time to research and raise these concerns about my client's proposal, but the fact of the matter is that nothing in Folly's zoning code and no state regulation would prohibit my clients from doing exactly what they have planned for the property."

Rosen paused for effect and then nodded his head slightly. "So, unless we want our next meeting to be held in a court of law, I respectfully request that your zoning commission grant the final approval of my client's proposal, that City Council ratify that approval, and that Folly deliver the necessary permits to my clients on Monday two weeks from this date by 9:00 a.m."

Check...

The silence was deafening. The next sound we heard was the voice of Bob Linville, a local businessman (later mayor) who said, "Yeah, I've been trying to figure out why we're having these meetings anyway. These guys want to spend several million dollars on Folly Beach and Beck's talking about the quality of life. What's that got to do with anything?" This episode was the first of many times that Bob Linville and I would disagree over development vs. quality-of-life issues.

The permits were issued on the date Morris requested. Our group huddled together over a pitcher of beer trying to figure out what our next move would be. We didn't have a Plan B, but we eventually decided that if we couldn't stop the project legally, we would do everything within our power to create negative publicity about it. John Manzi scheduled a local television station to come out and discuss the reasons this development was a bad idea.

Then the universe smiled. The day that John was scheduled to meet with the television people was blustery. The combination of a perigean tide and frisky northeast winds produced what we now call a "king tide." Luckily, the peak of that tide coincided with John's scheduled interview. The visual that appeared on television was of John expressing his concerns on one side of the "coming development" sign and the reporter on the other. It was a tight shot that showed only the sign and the two of them from the waist up. When the piece ended, the camera panned back to show them standing in water almost knee deep with parts of the property behind them being overtopped by the ocean.

It was a perfect video moment for us.

Checkmate!

In the end, Columbia Management never sold enough units to be a success. The company bought a lot on West Ashley, sold its model home, and left Folly, subsequently developing a similar, though smaller, development (also called Sea Cabins) on the commercial district beachfront of the Isle of Palms. That development still graces the shoreline on Isle of Palms and when I see it, I am once again grateful for that king tide.

About six weeks after Columbia Management left Folly, Dwight Moody of First Citizens Bank met with John, Rogers, Larry and me. He wanted to know if we thought there were other kinds of development that might be appropriate for that piece of property. We said we couldn't think of anything that would be permanent. Soon after, City Council began negotiations with First Citizens Bank and SCPRT, which had previously come to the city in 1977 with the idea of developing of a state park but had been unsuccessful.

Council was skeptical. A majority of the City Council thought that a state park was a bad idea because it removed a sizable piece of property from the tax rolls and a referendum had gone against a similar concept four years earlier. City Council negotiated permission from the South Carolina Department of Transportation (SCDOT) to restrict parking to the south side of West Ashley Avenue to help offset the additional traffic that would be generated by the visitors to the park.

A deal was eventually struck. SCPRT promised that the city could share revenue from the park but later reneged. SCPRT became the Charleston County Parks and Recreation Commission (PRC), which developed the area as a public park with two permanent shelters, rest rooms and changing areas, a snack bar, and public parking. The park quickly became one of Charleston's favorites, but erosion gradually endangered the permanent structures and parking.

The park continued to be damaged by erosion until PRC piggybacked on Folly's first renourishment, which occurred in 1992. The Corps of Engineers used sand from the Folly River to renourish the entire length of Folly, including the county park. That same year, PRC succeeded in permitting the placement of a sand-filled tube, 800 feet long and 12 feet in diameter, that was designed to project out into the ocean on the western edge of the property. The structure, known as a *terminal groin*, was designed to help retain subsequent renourishment. Construction was never started, and the permit was allowed to expire.

In 2011, Hurricane Irene caused so much erosion at the park that the ocean reached the structures, which had to be removed. PRC reapplied for the permit to build the terminal groin in 2014, but Dana Beach and the South Carolina Coastal Conservation League (SCCCL) blocked the permit over concerns about possible damage to the rookery at Bird Key. After PRC promised it would be responsible for the mitigation for any damages the project might cause, SCCCL withdrew its objection, and the groin was permitted. PRC placed the groin at the westernmost point of the property, nourished the beach with sand taken from the Folly River, and built new shelters at the park.

As of this writing, the renourishment at Folly Beach County Park and the rookery on Bird Key are both doing well. The west end of Folly Island remains a dynamic area. When I walk that beach today, I think of how different the situation would be now if, instead of a low-impact park enjoyed by tens of thousands of visitors each year, Folly was facing beleaguered homeowners trying to defend marginally-engineered structures on an eroding shoreline.

In April 1981, I proposed a height limitation ordinance (81-7) that would have set height limits not to exceed forty feet in Folly's commercial district and appeared before P&Z to urge its passage. However, P&Z, chaired by my adversary, Bob Linville, did not recommend my proposal to City Council. A majority of the council later blocked my attempt to introduce the ordinance a second time. The failure to pass that ordinance would have consequences just two years later

Chapter 9

Progress and Duplicity

In 1982, I ran for mayor for a second time against Lavern James and Wallace Benson. This time I won a decisive victory, garnering seventy percent of the votes in a runoff with Wallace.

In the first two years of my first term as mayor, I served with City Council members Dennis McKevlin, Larry Ridgeway, Don Singletary Jr., Gerald Davis, Francis Wilborn, and Fred Holland. I am in the center.

One of my first acts as mayor was to schedule a meeting with Frank Coggins Jr. of Coggins Land Development Corp. of Elberton, Georgia. He had recently purchased a part of Folly called Long Island and the property bordered by the seawall at the end of Center Street that now borders the County Fishing Pier, the Tides Hotel, and Oceanfront Villas.

The original Folly dance pier was built by Olaf Otto of Savannah and opened June 18, 1931. The adjacent pavilion was built by Ted

The Folly Beach Ocean Plaza under construction in 1959. *Wilbanks collection.*

An article in the *Folly Beachcomber* about the opening of the Plaza at which Mayor Riley's father officiated. (1960)

Shiadaressi in 1925. By 1936, Mr. Shiadaressi owned both structures. Both burned to the ground in 1957.

The second dance pier was rebuilt in 1959 at the same time as the development of the Folly Beach Ocean Plaza, which included a 1,700-foot concrete seawall that fronted the property. A small fishing pier was built to the east side of the dance pier by Jack Southworth and Michael Schultz in the early 1960s.

I spoke with my friend Dr. Gordan Stine, a dental educator, former county councilman, and an investor in the development partnership that built the Plaza. He called the Plaza Folly Beach's "tidepool of tears" because of all the money lost in the development's rapid descent into bankruptcy. By 1967, the original investors sold the property, at a loss, to Sea Point Corporation whose plans for the site did not materialize.

Then the property was sold to Gilead Christian Ministries, a corporation that represented the Folly Beach Baptist Church. Its development plans fell through and Royce Green bought it in 1980. Mr. Coggin's purchase of the property in 1981 set the stage for the developments that are protected by the seawall today.

That second dance pier burned in 1977, five years before my election as mayor. Years later, a gentle homeless man, Wolfman, told me he and a friend had improvised a rope ladder that let them access the pier after closing time. They secretly lived on the pier at night. Wolfman told me they had started a fire in the men's bathroom that had accidentally gotten out of control as they tried to stay warm after the pier closed on the very cold and snowy night of January 1, 1977.

Wolfman

The following images give a pictorial history of both dance piers, the 1970s fishing pier, and the conditions that existed when I took office as mayor in 1982.

The first Folly Beach dance pier in the early 1950s.
Wilbanks Collection

An aerial view of the Plaza property in the early 1960s. *Wilbanks Collection.*

The plaza and the second dance pier, built in 1959.
This photo was taken in the early 1960s.

Remains of the fishing and dance piers after they caught fire on January 1, 1977.

The remains of the Folly dance and fishing piers taken the morning after
the 1977 New Year's Day fire. *Richard Greene collection.*

Between the 1977 fire and my election as mayor, the area around what is now the PRC fishing pier deteriorated further and became increasingly dangerous. In 1979, Hurricane David destroyed the remains of the fishing pier and added that wreckage to the burned off pilings of the second dance pier.

Remains of the dance and fishing piers following Hurricane David in 1979.

When I met with Mr. Coggins, I shared my concern that the failing seawall, the remains of the piers, and the dilapidated buildings were a grave danger to the public. I was inclined to condemn the area but wanted to give him the opportunity to act before I did so.

Mr. Coggins wasn't happy about being pressured, but within six months he removed the old fishing pier and the remains of the dance pier. He destroyed all the buildings behind the seawall except for the one that now serves as the meeting hall for the Tides—and used the rubble from the demolished buildings as the base for a granite rip rap seawall.

It's still hard for me to believe that the original seawall built in 1960 was built so well, but the concrete seawall you see today, designed by Demitrios Liollio, extends some 30 feet into the beach surface. It is difficult to imagine now, but when I took office as mayor in 1982, some 25 feet of the seawall was exposed at low tide. The area was treacherous at most tides.

The following photos show the conditions at the base of the seawall in 1982, the condition of the abandoned buildings as they were being demolished, and the final protection of the concrete seawall with granite rocks. By the end of 1982, the entire area behind the seawall was ready for the future. And the future was not far behind.

Left: The seawall exposure at the west end of the Plaza seawall.

Right: The Plaza seawall exposure at the site of today's Tides swimming pool.

Condition of buildings at start of demolition.

The very precarious stairs to the beach.

West and east views of the stone-faced seawall

Get it in writing

In late 1982, Mr. Coggins sold the area that the Tides now occupies to Mr. Doug Allen. Doug was a local businessperson who had run a Pontiac dealership on Hwy. 17 and had built two Holiday Inns. He proposed building a Holiday Inn on Folly and brought to the table a preliminary commitment for a Community Development Block Grant to extend the sewer line from its Mariner's Cay terminus on the north side of the Folly River Bridge to the old Plaza property. City Council was universally in favor of bringing sewer to the commercial district.

Folly began working to secure the grant and making the sewer system a reality. The city's engineering firm proposed a grinder pump sewer system, perhaps the most expensive and maintenance-intensive system available. Fortunately, Folly had a resident, Gene Maree, who was a civil engineer. Largely thanks to Gene, City Council negotiated away from a grinder pump system to a more economical choice called a forced main system.

At the time, South Carolina law required that no matter what the circumstance, no sewer system could be installed in a community without the approval of its citizens in a binding referendum. The citizens of Folly in 1983, like the ones in 1972, were distrustful of their government and so concerned that a sewer system would bring high density development and expansion of the commercial district, that the first referendum attempt failed.

To answer residents' concerns about the spread of sewer and the scale of development, Larry Ridgeway and I convinced a majority of the council to amend the referendum question to stipulate that any future expansion of the system could occur only if that expansion was approved by a binding referendum. With that stipulation in place (ordinance 83-7), the permission to bring sewer to Folly passed in May 1983. Sewer was on the way to the commercial district.

Referendum Requirement Challenged

Not everyone was pleased with the limitation on future expansions of the sewer system. Three years later, in January 1985, Councilman Elliot Constantine and a group of citizens that called themselves "Friends of Folly" were unhappy because the requirement was interfering with plans for developing a project they favored called the Seabrook Tract. The group obtained enough signatures to force City Council to hold a third referendum in which they proposed that the requirement that a referendum precede any expansion of the system be repealed. The proposal was defeated by a two to one margin on April 29 of that year.

The 1977 zoning update, which had no height limits island wide, still controlled the zoning on Folly in 1983. My attempt to have City Council set height limits in 1981 had failed (ordinance: 81-7), and some of us feared the worst. Doug Allen made us feel better when he presented his plan for the new Holiday Inn. He proposed and presented drawings to illustrate two five-story towers with a public park between them that would allow pedestrian access to the vista of the open ocean and preserve the traditional view down Center Street to a limitless horizon.

The night in May of 1983 that the sewer referendum passed, Doug invited me, my fiancée Nancy Baldrick, City Council, and several other people who had been involved to his home on the Stono River.

Shortly after I arrived, Doug walked up and apologized, saying. "Richard, man, I am so sorry. I have been so busy lately that I haven't had a chance to talk to you about the changes that we had to make to our original proposal for the Inn." I had a really bad feeling as I was led to a small room, where he presented drawings that depicted a nine-story monolith in lieu of the twin mid-rise towers with a public park that he had promised. He said, "Yeah, unfortunately we miscalculated the footprint of two buildings and had to change our plans from two buildings to one."

My first helping of developer duplicity had been served. Live and learn. The failure of City Council to pass the height ordinance 81-7 came to mind. When I got back to the main room, I heard, "Who's up for skinny dipping in the pool?" I noticed that the TV was featuring questionable content and turned to Nancy.

"If we aren't out of this house in thirty seconds," I said, "it will be because you tripped. Get your things."

A cartoon by Rogers Oglesby gave voice to our collective fears.

Chapter 10

Opponents

I should have written this history in 2012. If I had, I could have talked to the principal players in this drama about their motivations. From this point on in the story, I was the mayor of a community that divided into two factions over which of the two visions of the community's future would prevail. Would it be slow growth, small buildings, low density, and an emphasis on owner occupation—or the opposite? Because many of the key players have passed on, I can only surmise what their motives were. Forty years later, there are some things that are clear to me and some that I still don't understand.

The majority of the community (myself included) felt that the tall buildings and high-density development, favored by a majority of City Council, were something to be avoided at all costs. Our reticence was not so much a result of having a clear vision of the future as much as it was a visceral reaction to a future of unbridled growth as simply wrong for the community.

The citizens that ultimately overwhelmed the then political majority found great solace in the intangibles that accompanied living in a small, largely forgotten seaside paradise and didn't want that quality of life to change. We could not imagine that adding more people, more traffic, and taller buildings would do anything but hasten the loss of tranquility and sense of community we so treasured. We saw less as more.

During this period of upheaval, we humorously referred to our side as the "Powers of Light" and the other side as the "Powers of Darkness."

That's not fair, but it's that kind of binary thinking that is both tempting and efficient when describing two groups whose goals are so far apart.

I believe that the people in this story who embraced tall buildings and high density were simply acting, as happens to this very day, to perpetuate the idea that all growth is good. The zoning plan passed in 1977 supported their perspective that a more vital business community, modernization, more tax revenue, and improved standing in the community at large were reasonable things to pursue.

Mostly, the old guard on Council were people who had lived on Folly and had controlled the levers of politics for a long time. The people of the Council and the business community had spent many years in a small beach town considered unworthy by the greater Charleston community. They had been longing for the kind of changes being offered and deeply resented any attempt to block the realization of that vision. The two groups did not value the same things and both sides took the disagreement personally.

Because the two sides could not see a suitable compromise, neither tried to communicate. I cannot remember ever offering or being offered a compromise. They vilified us as power hungry, and anti-progress. We kept asking them to do their jobs and give the community a chance to voice its desire. It was a stressful time, as continuous contention always is, but we were confident that the result of our efforts would be worth the stress and criticism were experiencing. We would not be the first to blink.

There is only one thing that, no matter how hard I try, I will never understand about our opposition: Why didn't they modify their obstructive positions when faced with votes on critical and relevant issues that went two to one against them? Why did they refuse to let the community have a voice? As events progressed, how did they not see what was happening? I believe they thought they would eventually prevail through conventional paths of power. They underestimated the will of their opponents.

Chapter 11

Losing the Dumbwaiter and Andre's Death

The first incident that indicated how seriously divided the community was over differing visions for Folly's future began innocently enough. In August 1983, City Council (me included) rezoned the Dumbwaiter property at the north foot of the bridge to Folly from residential to commercial. It felt like a reasonable thing to do as the area had always been used commercially.

In my childhood, this property had been the site of Andre's Restaurant and Tackle Shop. After Andre's death (at the hands of his wife), his restaurant was sold to Bobby Rabon in 1971 and became the Dumbwaiter. Bobby sold the bar to Perry O'Rourk in 1979. With Perry as owner, the Dumbwaiter became one of the locals' favorite bars and restaurants.

The Dumbwaiter

The Dumbwaiter occupied an older six-room house with a wide porch facing the river that was shaded most of the afternoon by a giant old oak tree. The porch overlooked an oyster shell beach with a small fishing pier. It was a perfect place for people to enjoy their drinks and the blessings of the afternoon sea breeze. The Dumbwaiter had great food. Two of its specialties were grouper cheeks and Vivian Taylor's crab cakes. Any time you walked in, you were likely to find Vivian's husband Nathan drinking a beer and picking crab at a table close to the bar. An order of Vivian's crab cakes, a little Tabasco sauce, an ice-cold beer, and a seat on the porch with a friend overlooking the river could melt away any care.

One day the Dumbwaiter was there and the next it was gone—crushed and carted off to clear the lot. Unwittingly, we had accelerated the developer's plans for the property, but we had no idea what those plans were. The sudden loss of the Dumbwaiter was an inflection point for many. Many people felt like a part of their heart had been ripped out. Losing this treasured restaurant helped people realize that if the people of Folly didn't try to control the fate of their community, it would end up like every other over-developed seaside town where developments are named after things that no longer exist.

Promise Her Anything But Take Her To . . .
ANDRE'S SEAFOOD RESTAURANT
Folly Road at Folly River
Specializing in
FRESH SEAFOOD–STEAKS–CHICKEN
Also Serving
ROASTED OYSTERS IN THE SHELL
— OPEN —
MON. THRU FRI.: 4:30 PM–11 PM   SAT.: 12–11 PM   SUN.: 12–9 PM

The Story of Andre's Death

Andre's death is an interesting bit of Folly's history and worth repeating. According to his wife's testimony at her trial for murder in 1970, Barbara Louise and Andre Marcel Thevenot had been happily married since 1936. In 1963, Andre hired June Cromeans as a waitress and hostess at the couple's restaurant, above which Andre and Barbara lived. Andre struck up a friendship with June that turned into an affair, which Mrs. Thevenot said, "made a nervous wreck of me."

Mrs. Thevenot testified that on May 1, 1969, Andre moved out of their house to live in a trailer next door to the Cromean trailer after Andre caught her in a motel room with another man. Barbara said that he was "just a good customer having a couple of drinks with her." Andre filed for divorce claiming adultery.

On October 23, Andre and June came over to the restaurant together after hours, and Barbara ordered June out of her house. June refused to leave. Barbara then went into her bedroom to call her lawyer, who instructed her to call the police. While making the call, she grabbed a handgun she had hidden at her bedside. Andre and June came into the room and tried to keep her from calling the police. At one point, she said, Andre hit her on the head with a bottle. During the struggle, Andre Thevenot was accidentally shot in the chest and died. He was 63.

The police testified as to what they found at the scene and informed the jury of Barbara's bruises from that evening's altercation. Barbara was acquitted because she was the only available eyewitness to the incident. The only other witness, June Cromeans, returned to Scotland with her husband shortly after the death of her lover.

Chapter 12

How to Win a War Without Winning a Battle
January 1984–September 1986

In January 1984, Realtec, a division of Continental Southeastern Group, outlined plans for a 440-unit, $24 million equestrian complex on the Seabrook Tract, a 57-acre parcel zoned PRD. It was bounded by 2nd Street West from Indian to Hudson, including what is now Lempisis Lane and the area of the West Ashley 6th Street cul-de-sac. The corporation also proposed a 350-unit expansion of Mariner's Cay east of Folly Road into Blacky's Campground (now Little Oak Island). In addition, Realtec announced plans for a thirty-seven room Mariner's Inn where the Dumbwaiter had existed.

A lot of changes were planned for our island and the residents got nervous. Having a nine-story Holiday Inn rather than the twin five-story hotel and public park, as promised, had been an education in how much they could trust a developer.

So much was happening so fast that people were overwhelmed and weren't sure what they could do to have an impact. As the mayor, I felt I had a mandate to limit high-density development on Folly and to promote Folly as a family-oriented, residential community. Councilman Larry Ridgeway shared my attitude, but was the only other member of Council that did. The other five members of City Council welcomed the new plans for development without reservation.

The Pivotal Election of May 1984

Besides the unveiling of the developer's plans mentioned above, several significant things happened in the three months before the May 1984 election that both energized and divided the community and resulted in outcomes that still define Folly Beach today.

January saw Realtec's attempt to ensure its ability to develop the Seabrook Tract by trying to sidestep the requirement that voters approve any expansion of the sewer system beyond the commercial district. Realtec offered to pay $50,000 for the sewer connection to the Holiday Inn if the referendum requirement was waived. The offer was not accepted, but the citizens took note.

In February, Larry Ridgeway resigned from his council seat four months before his term ended and moved from Folly to relocate his business. It was a blow to me, as I had come to depend on Larry as a steadfast soldier in the fight for low density.

The first piling for the nine-story Holiday Inn was driven on March 8, just six weeks before the groundbreaking for the sewer system, which occurred on April 29. These two events so close together were stark reminders that we would see a monolithic building blocking the view of the ocean at the end of Center Street in short order.

On Wednesday, March 7, I held a town hall meeting. Given everything happening in the community, I wanted to sample as wide a base as possible by holding a town meeting about development. The Community Center was packed.

I said that sewer availability was now a reality, and that, with our zoning laws as permissive as they were and with the majority of City Council favoring high-density development, rapid growth with unrestricted height was likely to be our destiny. I explained that I

Driving the first Holiday Inn piling, 1984.

wanted to prevent that kind of growth and noted that I was there to learn how people felt about the community's future.

The first person who asked to be recognized to speak was Rogers Oglesby. Unbeknownst to me, he was ready with a bombshell that would forever change Folly's history and would launch an 18-month battle between the community and the majority of City Council.

In researching the 1975 Home Rule Act of South Carolina, Rogers had found the Initiative and Referendum component (5-17-10), which allows the electorate to propose city ordinances through the presentation of petitions containing the signatures of 15 percent of the registered electors as of the last election. He wanted to use voter initiatives to propose two changes to our zoning ordinance.

The first petition supported an ordinance that would set a community-wide height limitation of 40 feet from ground level. Rogers explained that it was City Council's refusal to set height limits in 1981 that allowed the construction of the nine-story Holiday Inn.

The second petition supported an ordinance to change the zoning of the Seabrook Tract, which was slated for a large development. Rogers proposed that the tract be rezoned from PRD to single family residential (SFR)—a considerable downzoning because PRD allowed such a large variety of densities, uses, and configurations.

Before the town meeting, Rogers had gathered signatures on the two petitions and planned to propose the two changes to City Council as soon as possible. He also suggested that the people assembled that day meet two weeks later to start a new organization called the Folly Island Resident's Association (FIRA) to further this and other community causes. The audience was in general agreement and FIRA was born.

In early May 1984, Rogers Oglesby, as president of FIRA submitted the two petitions and their related ordinances to City Council—and expected the members to have them certified and either pass them or schedule binding referenda in compliance with state law. No action was taken by the council. None.

The Home Rule Act (5-17-10) gave City Council three options for reacting to ordinances sanctified by a petition under the Initiative and Referendum article: pass ordinances in substantial compliance with the FIRA proposals, schedule binding referendums on the FIRA proposals, or wait for up to a year to hold binding referendums on the FIRA proposals.

The Visionary Effect

FIRA's proposal to set a forty-foot height limit in the commercial districts in May of 1984 had immediate effects. I invoked the pending ordinance doctrine and let it be known that the building inspector would not consider buildings at heights above the proposed forty-foot limit. The height ordinance proposal prevented a bid by Doug Allen Jr. to develop a six-story condominium development on the east side of the Holiday Inn, where the PRC fishing pier now stands. It stopped a ten-story condominium development proposal by the Weathers family for the Sandbar Restaurant property. In 1985, the proposed ordinance squashed a scheme to build three twelve-story towers and an offshore swimming pool where the Oceanfront Villas is now located.

Think for a moment about how different Folly would be today if those projects (and possibly others) had not been blocked by Rogers's actions.

City Council's refusal to act on the ordinance proposals not only gave FIRA the moral high ground—giving substance to the threat that FIRA had expressed—but also vividly clarified the community's choices and piqued the village's interest in the May 1984 election.

The majority of the City Council seemed offended that this "upstart" organization would presume to change the normal top-down flow of power in the community. They maintained that FIRA was a loud-mouthed minority group and did not represent the community's wishes.

Their refusal to give the community a chance to express its wishes promptly pushed more of the community into FIRA's camp. FIRA, in fact, *did* represent what the community wanted, and the denial of the community's right to be heard eventually led to the majority's downfall.

Fury became the word of the day. The majority of the City Council was furious about being challenged, as was much of the community. The developers were furious at the possibility that a legal process might delay or prevent the development of their projects. Meanwhile, the minority on the City Council, whose view was that the community's wishes should be heard on these two ordinances remained resolute.

The May 1984 Election

Not surprisingly, the May 1984 City Council election was hotly contested. Eleven people ran for three council seats, including Doug Allen, Jr, one of Folly's newest residents and *the son of the developer of the Holiday Inn*. I publicly favored John Manzi, Wayne Hembree, and Dale Walworth, all of whom were active in FIRA.

John won outright, but Wayne, Gerald Davis and Elliot Constantine ended up in a runoff for the two remaining spots. Wayne and Elliot were elected to four-year terms. Two more years were left in my first term as mayor and the terms of councilpersons Francis Wilborn, Fred Holland, and Dennis McKevlin.

John Manzi and I had been good friends since 1978, had very similar attitudes about growth, and had worked together on various projects in the late 1970s and early 1980s. Wayne Hembree had been active in FIRA and was the only other person on the new council interested in limiting growth and setting height limits. Rogers was busy growing FIRA into a substantial grass roots organization. The pro-development sentiments of Fred, Francis, and Dennis were well-known because of their resistance to height limitations in 1981 and to sewer restrictions in 1983. Elliot's sentiments aligned with theirs. It was four against three: McKevlin, Wilborn, Constantine and Holland against Beck, Manzi and Hembree.

The 1984 City Council: Fred Holland, John Manzi, Francis Willborn, me, Wayne Hembree, Dennis McKevlin, and Elliot Constantine.

Many events followed in quick succession:

- Council's refusal to act on the ordinances that FIRA had proposed did not prevent me from having the two petitions certified and reintroducing them to City Council for passage as ordinances 84-14 and 84-15. They were referred to P&Z. Under Chairman Linville, P&Z held public hearings but recommended against adoption of the ordinances to City Council. The majority of the new City Council agreed with the P&Z's conclusions and expressed their intention to do nothing further.

- On July 11, Realtec, exercised an option to purchase the Seabrook Tract—the option was purchased one month and five days after the petition to change its zoning was first presented to City Council.

- On July 17, in an effort to force action by Council, I reintroduced the two ordinances that FIRA had created. Elliot Constantine introduced a motion to not only table further discussion of the ordinances but to "keep them tabled." His motion passed 4 −3.

- At the August 7 meeting, City Council revived and passed the first reading (three readings are required for passage) of FIRA's height ordinance and amended the forty-foot height limitation ordinance introduced by FIRA to fifty feet. The second and third readings never happened because they were blocked by Council's minority.

- On August 10, FIRA sued in general sessions court asking the court to force City Council to set a date to hold a binding referendum on the zoning of the Seabrook Tract.

- On August 16, FIRA sued asking for an injunction against the granting of permits for the Seabrook Tract.

- On August 29, P&Z held a midweek, mid-morning meeting to review Realtec's plans for the Seabrook Tract. The timing of the meeting purposefully excluded any possibility of my attendance.

- On September 5, P&Z submitted a conditional plat approval for the Seabrook Tract to City Council although many legally required details of the developer's application were missing. City attorney, Ben Peeples, reminded the P&Z Board that the developer's need to satisfy the requirements of Folly's subdivision ordinance was not optional and that one requirement was providing sewerage. Since the provision of sewerage outside of the commercial district was subject to referendum, it was impossible to guarantee this requirement. Four months later, Elliot Constantine and the Friends of Folly lost their bid to overturn the ordinance requiring a successful referendum before expansion of the system by a margin of two to one.

- On September 13, Judge Fields refused to block the permits to Realtec and refused to force the referendum required by the Home Rule Act. FIRA appealed.

- On October 26, Realtec applied for a permit to construct an access road to begin the development of the Seabrook Tract. The building official, Ed Wilder, referred the request to the P&Z board, which approved the request and sent it back to Ed to grant the permit.

- In November, FIRA asked Judge Richard Fields to prevent the issuance of a permit to build this road until the requirements of the Home Rule Act were satisfied. That decision was under consideration as the next five months passed.

The past enables the present

You will recall that in 1976, Folly had changed its method of governance from the weak mayor form to the strong mayor form. The strong mayor form of governance gives the mayor robust responsibility for and control over the execution of city ordinances and state law through the city's employees. The only employees *not* under the direct control of the mayor are the city clerk, judge, and attorney, all of whom work for the majority of City Council.

After the October 26 request for an access road was reviewed and approved by the P&Z board, it was our building inspector Ed Wilder's responsibility to issue the permit. The court was still considering FIRA's request that the judge block that very permit. Ed called me when the request hit his desk. We reviewed the developer's overall plan for compliance with our subdivision ordinance and unlike the P&Z board, we found it incomplete.

My biggest concern was that if our building official issued any permit without satisfying the requirements of both the initiatives that FIRA had legally proposed, and the requirements of our subdivision ordinance; state and local law would be violated, and FIRA petitioners would be denied due process.

I sought legal counsel and, once again, implemented the legal tool called the "pending ordinance doctrine." I instructed the building inspector to deny any permits that would advance the development of the Seabrook Tract because there was a FIRA ordinance in process (pending) that would make the proposed development impossible.

Ed denied the permit. Ten days later, when the developer sought an injunction to force Folly to grant the permit, I was sitting in Justice Field's courtroom with my right hand on a Bible swearing to tell the truth. I was not nervous. I was determined. I testified that my instructions to Mr. Wilder were based on three things.

I argued that FIRA had submitted a legally binding petition and that the corresponding ordinance was in place to change the zoning of the Seabrook Tract before the developer's exercise of its option to buy the tract or its application for site plan approval. Ordinance (84-15) had started a legislative process that included up to a year during which it would either be passed or a binding referendum held. I maintained that as the proscribed process was not complete, and that, when it was, the zoning of the property might change, rendering the developer's proposal moot.

I also pointed out that the developer had not complied with our subdivision ordinance, which required specific plans for sewer service. I reminded the court that Folly already had an ordinance (83-7) that required that an expansion of the sewer system beyond the existing commercial district could be done only after approval via a referendum. Since the property was outside of the commercial district, it was impossible to present a legitimate plan for plat approval until the question of whether sewer would be extended to the property was answered.

As far as I was concerned, until the city either passed a law in substantial compliance with the petition-supported ordinance or held a binding referendum on the ordinance proposed by FIRA, issuing any permit would violate the community's right to due process.

The developer sued me and Folly for the access road and plan approval, saying, ironically enough, that while the letter of the law gave City Council up to a year to make a decision, City Council's expressed desire to postpone that referendum for the entire year had rendered the law fatally flawed. The developer argued that it was unreasonable to expect them to wait a year for resolution and being forced to wait violated *their* rights to due process. In other words, as we began the court battle, the developer, and I (FIRA) were *both* defending the right to due process.

The rubber meets the road

Recall that City Council had three options for reacting to ordinances sanctified by a petition under the Initiative and Referendum article of the Home Rule Act: 1) pass ordinances in substantial compliance with the FIRA proposals, 2) schedule binding referendums on the FIRA proposals, or 3) do nothing and wait for up to a year to hold binding referendums on the FIRA proposals.

The majority of City Council chose to wait the year and hope that its inactivity would help the developer's case prevail. As a result, two legal questions became the focus of the controversy. One, if City Council did nothing for a year, did the developer's right to due process trump the due process that the enforcement of the initiative and referendum section of the Home Rule Act afforded the citizens? And two, did the Initiative and Referendum section of the Home Rule Act itself violate the division of responsibility that normally surrounds the process of deciding zoning questions?

The developer claimed that City Council had the authority to act as it saw fit with respect to zoning and that questions of zoning should not be subject to the initiative and referendum rules, despite what the state law said.

The applicability of the sewer access question somehow got lost because the battle centered immediately on the permit for road access, and although access to sewer was a question that had to be answered, it never became an issue disputed in court.

The majority on City Council soon concluded that in addition to taking no action on FIRA's ordinance proposals, it would also instruct the city attorney not to offer a defense (of the city and me) against the developer's suit, thereby assuring the developer's success.

Only one thing stood in the way. To formally instruct the city attorney not to defend the mayor's position required a vote to do so in a regularly scheduled council meeting. As the minority of City Council, it became John's, Wayne's and my job to make sure that the vote never happened.

An ethical bind

Because the mayor's position differed from the desire of the majority of City Council and the city attorney works for the majority, Ben was in a bind. Should he defend the position that I took as mayor or uphold the council majority's preference, no matter how unexpressed it might be?

Peeples mostly laid low, recognizing that his ethical duty lay with the wishes of the majority on City Council even if it had not been formally expressed. But he also knew that if FIRA obtained standing, it could argue my position even if he couldn't. In the interest of what lawyers call the doctrine of fairness, he found FIRA an excellent attorney, Robert (Bob) Haley, and helped FIRA obtain legal standing in the case. Gedney Howe III represented the developer.

Attorneys must be be paid, so FIRA became a 501(c)(3) non profit and began fundraising. With Rogers as its leader, FIRA published *The Tideline*, a monthly newsletter, and raised money through bake sales, garage sales, oyster roasts, and individual contributions. FIRA successfully raised the funds needed to pay Mr. Haley through the year and a half that the issue was in court.

The minority finds a way

Still, as the minority, we had to be strategic. To protect FIRA's right to due process, we had to keep City Council from voting on any part of the permit issue or formally instructing the city attorney to cease his defense of the city. Every meeting was a struggle, but the minority eventually kept the majority from voting on anything concerning the lawsuit. We implemented the tried and true, last-resort tool of the minority—the filibuster, a procedural means of stopping debate on a motion where opponents of the motion hold the floor with discussion until the other side gives up and agrees to table the motion, which prevents its passage.

Our strategy (and ultimate success) was based on ideas from a book that was popular at the time, John Nesbit's *Megatrends* (1982). Chapter 7, "From Representative Democracy to Participatory Democracy," explains the importance of voter initiatives. John, Rogers, Wayne, and I decided this chapter would be our justification and our tool for controlling the actions of City Council regarding the lawsuit.

A motion to aid the developer and instruct the city attorney was on several City Council agendas that year. As the mayor, it was my rules of order privilege to set the order of the agenda in advance and to choose who was to speak first whenever a motion came to the floor. That power helped me and my two allies prevent any vote that would have harmed FIRA's defense of my position.

Whenever a motion concerning the Seabrook Tract or a motion to instruct the city attorney made it to debate, I would ask John or Wayne to speak first. They would explain why they thought the motion was on the agenda and the problems with City Council's failure to honor the call for an immediate referendum. Then either John or Wayne would reference a national trend that supported FIRA's role as an example of legitimate participatory democracy. Next they would point out that a current national best-selling author, John Nesbit, spoke to our point.

John or Wayne would then ask me if it would be okay to read a little from Chapter 7 of *Megatrends* to help City Council understand that legitimacy and I would respond, "Please do." They would then begin reading and after a page or two, I would interrupt and say that I hoped that the importance of what they were reading wasn't lost on the majority and then ask them to please reread the passage to further emphasize the point. Our filibusters never lasted over twenty minutes before the opposition would give up.

I remember that Elliot Constantine, who was refreshingly unscripted and colorful, collaring me after a meeting and saying, "Richard, do you know what your problem is? You don't understand democracy. We have four votes, you have three. We are going to win." My response was, "Well, maybe—but then again—you might be surprised."

Let's try this

Frustrated by the minority's ability to filibuster its way to victory, the majority tried another tack. In January 1985, well into the fight, Councilman Fred Holland proposed that the Council's rules of order be amended so that the number of members sufficient for a quorum would be reduced from five to four. The goal was to call a meeting at a time when I could not attend, which would allow the majority to prevail. The minority prevented this from happening in our usual manner. We filibustered the motion with the same arguments.

In the middle of all this

In January 1985, Frank Coggins Jr. sought a Coastal Council permit to rebuild the old toll road causeway between Oak Island and Long Island—to gain road access to Long Island. A year earlier, Folly's City Council had forever alienated Oak Island by passing a resolution (84-3) that supported rebuilding the bridge that once connected Oak Island to Long Island as part of the old toll road to Folly Beach.

The Coastal Council's public hearing for the permit application to rebuild the causeway and bridge was one of the most enjoyable I have ever attended. The people of Oak Island were having none of it because rebuilding the causeway would make their quiet community the gateway to developing Long Island.

They were both articulate and witty in their opposition. At one point, the attorney for Mr. Coggins said, "Wait a minute. Now I understand. You've got my client all wrong. He's not a developer; he's an environmentalist. He doesn't want to rebuild the causeway to develop the island. He wants to rebuild the causeway to re-establish the bald eagle habitat there." The audience laughed long and hard. Their response was priceless and the permit was denied.

That same year, Janette Stevenson, head of Atlantic Brokerage Co., a subsidiary of Coggins Enterprises Inc., revealed its plans for the Breakwater Condominiums. The design featured three 12-story towers and an offshore swimming pool. When Ms. Stevenson announced the project, she said that the property was not large enough for the three condominium buildings *and* the pool—hence the offshore pool. Thankfully, Rogers's proposed ordinance to set a height limit of 40 feet in the commercial district activated the pending ordinance doctrine, which, when combined with the improbability of securing permission to construct an offshore swimming pool, made the success of this proposal unlikely. Without the support of Coastal Council, the project made no real headway.

Rendering of the Breakwater in 1985

FIRA was quick to point out that this proposal illustrated the problems we could face without height limitations in the commercial district. Rogers Oglesby, a skilled cartoonist, created a wonderful poster that illustrated the absurdity of the proposal and the threat it represented.

Falling Dominos

As the minority held off the majority of council, Bob Haley was working on the legal end with Ben assisting within the bounds of his ethical constraints. Although Haley mounted a spirited defense of the position I had taken, the developer won at every court level. While we wished our prospects looked more promising, we held fast to this

Rogers Oglesby cartoon, 1985

consolation: as long as court hearings were taking place, no building was taking place. FIRA defended the lawsuit against the city and funded every appeal necessary.

Then, suddenly, legal action by the developer's creditors took center stage away from the court proceedings. Early in 1985, Stockton Savings and Loan foreclosed on the Seabrook Tract and became the plaintiff in the suit between Folly Beach, FIRA, and the former developer. Other financial realities dictated the course of events. The Federal Home Loan Bank Board foreclosed on all other properties owned by Realtec on both sides of Folly Road. Although the original developer was winning its legal battle, it was losing its financial battle—the house of cards was collapsing.

The full scope of their county-wide unpaid financial obligations became public. Many of those unmet obligations were to local contractors, including those working on Mariner's Cay Racquet and Yacht Club and there were hundreds of liens on multiple properties throughout Charleston County. Later, the individual owners of the Mariner's Cay condos discovered that money that should have funded the horizontal property regime was missing.

Then, in April 1985, Judge Richard Fields issued an order that would have forced the city to grant the permit to build the entrance road into the Seabrook property development. However, by that time, Realtec was out of the picture. Stockton Savings and Loan now controlled all that corporation's assets. FIRA appealed Judge Field's order and Stockton Savings and Loan appealed to the South Carolina Supreme Court, which rendered a decision on the case in September 1986, almost a year and a half after the original developer had gone bankrupt.

I am told by attorneys that after the arguments, counter arguments, and minutiae that go into arguing a case, rulings in supreme courts are usually decided on very narrow grounds and so it would be. On September 22, 1986, in *Continental Southeastern Group v. City of Folly Beach*, the high court's ruling boiled down to four findings in a ruling that favored the developer:

1. The pending ordinance doctrine did not prevent the issuance of a road permit.
2. City Council's refusal to consider the ordinances promptly or to publically announce that they intended to pass the ordinances amounted to a failure to show any intent on its part to pass them.
3. The zoning of the Seabrook Tract that existed prior to the initiative that changed it to single family residential (SFR) would be restored to planned residential development (PRD) (The property had been zoned SFR on the same day that Rogers was elected to Council in August of 1985).
4. The court refused to consider any of the other issues brought before it.

The court either missed the point of the controversy or saw the future implications of the Initiative and Referendum section of the Home Rule Act and didn't want the concept of citizen initiatives to gain any credibility. Apparently, the authors of the 1975 Home Rule Act never anticipated that a city council would actually take an entire year to make a decision in the face of an issue with enough political legs to generate a successful petition drive and a formidable community presence. Folly's City Council had proven to the court that giving a city council as much as a year to delay deprived the developer of due process. Due process for the citizens wasn't even addressed.

The court decision weakened the ability of citizens to use the Initiative and Referendum approach to affect zoning. The decision implied that City Council members were more qualified to make decisions about zoning issues than a citizenry, although the Home Rule Act gave the citizens of a municipality that power. The court's assumption became the rule of law in *I'On, L.L.C. v. City of Mt. Pleasant* in 2001. Since then, zoning issues can no longer be the subject of a voter initiative. The power over zoning rests solely in the hands of the city council of each municipality.

That decision in the South Carolina Supreme Court, however, would prove to be 18 months too late to alter the fate of the Folly developer.

Persistence comes with benefits

Although I am sure that Elliot Constantine did not mean to give John Manzi a present, he did, resigning from Council for personal reasons on May 13, 1985, which happened to be John's birthday.

Ironically enough, the election to fill Elliot's unexpired term and the long-awaited binding referendum on changing the zoning of the Seabrook Tract were held on the same day. On Monday, August 5, Rogers Oglesby was elected to council over Gerald Davis by 438 to 224. By an almost exact duplicate vote of 435 to 202, the voice, so long denied the citizens of Folly, was finally heard and by a vote of two to one, the voters of Folly affirmed the FIRA-generated ordinance by eliminating the PRD zoning classification from Folly's zoning ordinance.

That September, City Council passed the 1984 FIRA-generated ordinance to limit height in the commercial district and amended the ordinance, returning to the originally petitioned 40 feet.

Not one of the Council people who comprised the majority during this period ran for reelection in the spring of 1986. I was opposed for reelection by Bob Linville but was easily elected to a second term as mayor. The members of City Council who had denied the community a referendum on ordinances—brought to them by earnest petition—were replaced with candidates more in favor of preserving the island's quality of life. In April 1986, Tommy Bolus, Marianne Read, and Rex Whitcomb were elected, joining Rogers Oglesby, Wayne Hembree, and John Manzi to serve with me on City Council.

Since PRD zoning had been eliminated in August 1985, the council's first order of business was to eliminate the other multi-family housing and high-density developments that our zoning ordinance allowed. We did. Except for the commercial district, the rest of Folly Island is still zoned as single-family today.

Shortly after the Supreme Court decision, Ravenel, Eiserhardt & Associates (represented by Sunday Lempesis and John Disher) optioned the Seabrook Tract from Stockton Savings and Loan and promised Folly a single-family development.

After their plans were developed and approved, the community voted in a special referendum on November 4, 1985. By a margin of two to one, voters approved the extension of sewer into the Seabrook Tract, opening the door for it to be developed as it is today—as a residential neighborhood with 183 single family homes.

The Realtec-planned 350-unit extension onto Little Oak was bought out of receivership and developed as single-family parcels, except for multi-family units already under construction. The Mariner's Inn, the site of Andre's, was demolished after being irrevocably damaged by Hurricane Hugo in 1989. In 2000, it was replaced by Turn of River Condominiums.

The majority of people on Folly Island had lost every battle...but had won the war. To read profiles of the people who played a major role in this community victory, please refer to the Appendix.

Rogers's vision realized

No city council, no matter how homogenous in attitude toward preserving the quality of life of a community, will see eye to eye on all subjects. Heated controversies continued in the years following the 1986 election.

To its credit, the City Council of 1986–1987 tightened up our zoning, put a lid on height and density, and put in place laws that have had an indelible effect on the community. Folly would be a different place if, among other things, popular activism hadn't been rallied to take control of our future. If Rogers Oglesby hadn't started those petitions...

There are so many ifs in the prospect of protecting what is unrecoverable if lost. If you live on an island with an embarrassment of riches, the challenges of controlling the quality and character of a community's growth are a matter of continued vigilance. The citizens of Folly Beach took bold actions to preserve their quality of life in the mid-1980s.

We are their beneficiaries today. Folly is one of the few beach communities in the United States that has kept its conservation character. This preservation is something to be proud of in these days of hypercommercialization, pollution, climate change denial, pressure to increase densities, and homogenization. If these challenges are not handled with diligence, they can easily leave a community like Folly with no connection to the spirit of the land and sea.

Following are photos of some of the key players and a *News and Courier* editorial that ran after we gained control of the council.

rials 14-A   **Democracy Triumphs In Folly Beach**

The News and Courier

The South's Oldest Daily Newspaper

leston, S.C., Friday, August 9, 1985   58 Pages   4 Sections   ★ ★ ★   25¢ Daily   Telephone 577-7111   Classified 722-6500 · Circulation · 722-2223

CHARLESTON, S.C., FRIDAY, AUGUST 9, 1985, PAGE 14-A

Triumph At Folly Beach

Some years ago, a group of residents began to feel that the future of Folly Beach was being shaped against the wishes of the majority by a few politicians who were backed by big developers. So they organized a grass roots organization called the Folly Island Residents' Association and set about to prove that government of the people, by the people, for the people has not perished from the earth.

Their battle was long and, at times, bitter. Time after time the members who represented the majority of the people were defeated when it came to voting on development projects on city council. It began to look as if the developers had Folly Beach sewn up. But the developers had not reckoned with the power of grass roots politics, nor, specifically, with a little known state law, in force since 1975 but never used before, which allows voters in municipalities to petition for a referendum to propose or modify ordinances.

It took over a year to get city council to agree to the referendum. The first task was securing the signatures of 15 percent of all registered voters on a petition to defeat a plan, approved by a 4-3 majority on the council, to build something called a planned urban development — a PUD is a mix of condomin-iums, multi-family housing and single-family homes — on 58 acres of the island and at the same time raise the building height limitation by 10 feet to 50 feet. The referendum was held on Monday and it resulted in a 2-1 victory over PUD, so that the area will have single-family homes, as well as the rejection of the 10-foot height increase. In an election held at the same time for a seat on the city council the candidate who had sided with the developers was also defeated. Over 50 percent of registered voters cast ballots in the referendum.

More than just a great victory for the majority of people in Folly Beach, who want to save the permanent things in their community that money can't buy but that uncontrolled development can destroy forever, the referendum was a reminder of the power of grass roots politics. Although South Carolinians have been denied state-wide voter initiatives on the lines of the various propositions which have had such an impact in other parts of the country, Folly Beach has shown that the people's will cannot be flouted all the time. It was about time that politicians were reminded that they are supposed to be the representives of the people, not spokesmen for powerful interests. The story of the Folly Beach voter initiative should reverberate around the state.

1985 editorial in the *News and Courier*

Me, Bill Griffin, Wayne Hembree, Rogers Oglesby, and John Manzi—all FIRA advocates.

Roger Oglesby's Election Day, August 5, 1985. Me, Susan Howell,
Rita Oglesby, Rogers Oglesby, Nancy Baldrick, Harriet McCutchen,
Francis Murphy, Oscar Oakes, Wes Murphy, Melody Murphy, and Dee Oakes—
all stalwarts in FIRA

Unearthing Our Past

In the spring of 1987, Civil War artifact enthusiasts Robert Bohrn and Eric Croen discovered a Civil War era burial on the land that was to be the roadbed of what was to be the extension of West Indian Avenue into the Seabrook Tract. An archaeological excavation was done by the University of South Carolina Institute of Archaeology and Anthropology under the guidance of its director, Steve Smith.

The study revealed 19 Civil War-era burials. The institute determined that the remains were in a brigade burial ground and that the soldiers were members of the "African Brigade" under the command of Gen. Edward A. Wild. The brigade was made up of former slaves serving in the 1st North Carolina and the Massachusetts 55th, which had replaced the Massachusetts 54th, and were part of the 13,000 Union troops stationed on Folly during the Siege of Charleston between November 1863 and February 1865. The remains were re-interred in the National Cemetery in Beaufort, SC. in 1988 with then-presidential candidate Michael Dukakis presiding.

Flag-draped caskets at the re-interment of unearthed remains at the Beaufort National Cemetery.

In May 1989, forensic artist Roy Paschal, formerly with the S.C. State Law Enforcement Division (SLED), created facial reconstructions of two of the soldiers whose remains were unearthed. The movie *Glory*, which depicts the sacrifices of the Massachusetts 54th Regiment in the battle for Morris Island (during the Siege of Charleston) came out that same year.

The Folly Beach Riverfront Park was dedicated to their memory in 2011 with an historical marker.

Bronze facial reconstructions by Roy Paschal. *Robert Bohrn collection.*

Chapter 13

Good Deeds Punished
1988

Following all the successes of FIRA and the City Council of 1984–1986, the cohesiveness of the FIRA coalition unraveled. We were shocked at the time but on reflection, I think that what happened to FIRA is what happens to a lot of grassroots movements. It is difficult for people to maintain the level of intensity required to make the changes we made in the face of stiff opposition.

People yearned for the bliss of the political ignorance they had enjoyed before the fight to preserve their quality of life. Just enough of the fighters lost interest that the balance shifted. The very individuals who had stood in the way of their vision found their way to back into power.

The election of May 1988 brought unexpected and unhappy surprises when Bob Linville, a longtime adversary of FIRA, was elected to the City Council. Bob had been a consistent adversary during the four-year battle to ward off development. Rogers Oglesby also lost his bid for a full term in a runoff to Penny Travis. Although Penny had worked in FIRA, she was a lot closer to Bob Linville than to me.

Rogers got another chance to secure a seat on the council in a special election in November 1988, after Wayne Hembree resigned to move to the northwest part of the state. The special election came down to a runoff between Rogers and Wallace Benson, one of my most vocal critics.

Wallace was the police chief that had resigned in 1980 and left the community without police or fire protection and had worked against funding the effort to prove the causal relationship between the jetties and erosion on Folly. I had beaten him twice for mayor in what were ugly campaigns. He was no fan of mine or what I considered the important accomplishments of the previous four years.

Rogers was the visionary behind forcing height limitations and drastically decreasing the density on Folly. And yet, after all that he had done to positively affect Folly's future, he would be subjected to a cruel twist of political fate.

A preview of hanging chads

For reasons of convenience and frugality, the local election was held on the same day as the national election that year. There was not enough room on the general election ballot for both the general and local elections, so Folly was forced to use paper ballots for the local election.

The local election could not have gone worse. You may remember that in November 2000, hanging chads played a crucial role in the presidential contest between George W. Bush and Al Gore. Folly was no better served by using paper ballots in 1988.

Folly's paper ballots were marked with a pen and as the ballot count proceeded, it became clear that there would be problems. There were ballots on which voters voted for both candidates. There were ballots cast by people not registered to vote. There were ballots where it was unclear which candidate a voter had chosen. After the initial count, 12 ballots were challenged (and not counted in the first tally). Rogers Oglesby led by one vote.

Naturally Wallace requested a recount, which meant that every ballot, challenged and unchallenged, would be closely scrutinized for a second time. Two days later, there was standing room only as the supporters of each candidate filled the stairway to the packed second floor of city hall where the recount was being held.

The recount began with the untallied contested ballots. Only one contested ballot was positively assigned. That ballot went to Wallace, which one would expect to produce a tie. But when the total ballot recount was finalized, the official count had Wallace ahead by one vote.

Rogers naturally asked, "How that could be? Where did the extra vote come from?" No one could explain what happened.

Following the count, Rogers filed a protest, but the election commission chairman, Bob Stoertz, had given him incorrect information about his rights with respect to filing a protest, and his protest was filed too late to be considered. The election commission informed Rogers that as far as it was concerned, the election was over. No avenue for appeal was available.

Rogers sued in the Court of Common Pleas and obtained an injunction that prevented Wallace from taking his seat on council until the matter was settled.

The election commission felt so bad that they had given Rogers poor information, they wrote the judge, Bruce Littlejohn, and told him about their error, expressed how sorry they were, and said that they felt like a new election should be held.

However, the judge gave no weight to their plea and refused to hear any witnesses. Then, in a turn of events that proved the old adage that no matter how consequential, "no good deed goes unpunished," the court awarded the election to Wallace.

Wallace had been prevented from taking the seat from November of 1988 until March 27, 1989. When he took his seat and joined Bob Linville, contention returned to the City Council.

We all were so disappointed, not only for Rogers but for what his loss meant to sound government. Rogers accepted the loss with grace, turned toward his business, and continued to advance his art career. He and Rita enjoyed the simple pleasures of retirement and continued to be active in the community as a force for protecting the quality of life for Folly's citizens.

It is said of "disrupters" like Rogers that those who may seem disruptive at first often open the way to thinking about a subject in a different way. Rogers was such a person. He was Folly's visionary.

Chapter 14

Renourishment: A Fifty-Year Commitment
1978–1986

This chapter is a "bookend" to the Introduction because what we set out to do—prove the causal relationship between the Charleston Harbor jetties and erosion on Folly Beach—spanned all 11 years I was in office. Thus far, I have described the steps of proving the connection in pieces—as each coincided with other political struggles—and as a result, may have made that singular accomplishment less obvious. Some information provided in earlier chapters is repeated here so the connections between the Charleston jetties and erosion on Folly—and our success in finally winning a 50-year commitment to beach renourishment—can be understood as a continuous narrative.

In May 1978, Bill Lee, chairman of Folly's first erosion committee, presented the results of its one-year study of possible courses of action to solve our severe erosion problem. I had just come onto City Council. I thought the report was fascinating and asked so many questions that I was appointed the chairman of a *new* erosion committee tasked with moving their efforts forward.

When I took over as chairman, City Council was in the midst of an ill-fated effort to sue the federal government for redress of our problems with erosion. I learned of the American Shore and Beach Preservation Association (ASBPA) and the Florida Shore and Beach Preservation Association (FSBPA), the mother lode of information on preserving beaches. I attended FSBPA's December 1978 meeting in Miami Beach and was introduced to Eric Olsen of Olsen and Associates of Jacksonville, Florida, a coastal engineer who had just worked with the Corps of Engineers to complete a study that connected the erosion of down-drift beaches to the jetty system at St. Mary's Inlet, Florida. (The US Navy had built the jetty system to maintain a navigable channel for the Mayport naval facility on the Georgia-Florida border.) I was also introduced to Dr. Robert Dean, considered the "dean" of coastal processes in the country.

They both assured me there was no way a lawsuit would force the federal government to do anything and that Folly would need to drop the lawsuit and let everyone save face, and then negotiate the beginning of a Section 1-11 review for our community. Section 1-11 (section 215 of public law 485) of the 1968 Rivers and Harbors Act (revised) is a provision that allows the federal government to mitigate damages caused by navigation projects to adjacent shorelines without admitting guilt.

Incredulous, City Council was not willing to drop the lawsuit or allow the committee to proceed. Folly's erosion problems were horrific at this point—as shown by these images.

Top: An eastern view from the east end of the seawall during the January 1, 1987 "No Name" Storm. **Bottom:** The "sandgrabber" was a device designed to slow down wave action and capture sand. Unfortunately, it was unsuccessful.

Failed seawalls on the 10th block of East Arctic.

Left: Center of old Plaza seawall. Right: 12th Street from the east, looking west.

The Plaza during a storm.

The remains of Benket Drive, which was constructed in 1962.
This photo was taken in 1986.

In early 1979, our state representative, Paul Gelegotis, had gotten the state to increase the state budget for shoreline needs from $150,000 to $600,000, $440,000 of which was allocated to Folly Beach to solve its erosion problem. It was the first time that any state money had been appropriated for erosion control other than for groin construction and maintenance.

In August 1979, Dr. John Manzi, a marine biologist and Folly resident, and Dr. Margaret Davidson, head of the Sea Grant Consortium, used their contacts with the National Science Foundation (NSF) to obtain a grant to fund a forum to help Folly determine the best use for that money. Through the NSF grant, we brought to the panel some of the most knowledgeable people in the country, including Dr. Miles Hayes (who, along with Dr. Tim Kana, had just published the first comprehensive work on coastal processes in our state), Dr. Robert Dean, Eric Olsen, Dr. Billy Edge, Dr. John Fisher, Dr. John Clarke, and several other major players in coastal processes in America, including representatives of the Charleston District of the U.S. Army Corps of Engineers. The forum was convened at the auditorium of the Fort Johnson Marine Research Institute on December 13, 1979.

The chief of planning at the local district office in Charleston was Mr. Edwin Meredith. Mr. Meredith and, as far as anyone could tell, all the career employees of the district Corps office and the entire Corps hierarchy, were adamant that the Charleston Harbor jetties had nothing to do with the erosion on Folly. They held to that position even though it was common knowledge that jetty systems one-tenth the size of the Charleston Harbor Navigation Project (CHNP) did exactly what our jetties do—prevent sand from passing the inlets they serve and starve the beaches that are downdrift of them. A bibliography that gave weight to that conclusion was assembled and distributed. In a September 22, 1978 editorial, the News and Courier had excoriated Folly's legislators for trying to get the public to share in the solution to Folly's problem. The newspaper maintained that position all the way through our fight to prove the causal relationship.

One outcome of the workshop was that every member of the committee agreed that the Charleston Harbor jetties contributed significantly to our erosion problem by blocking the littoral flow of sand. The question was not *if* but *how much*. The conference had three recommendations: 1) that Folly ask the Army Corps for a Section 1-11 review of the relationship between the Charleston jetties and erosion on Folly, 2) that the $440,000 should be escrowed until a renourishment project could be carried out or spent on a dune rebuilding and walkover construction project, and that 3) Folly establish a sovereignty line, or a division between public and private property that would be required before renourishment could begin.

In February of 1980, the proceedings and findings of the conference were presented to the South Carolina Coastal Council as the "Folly Beach Erosion Abatement Proposal."

The conclusions of the NSF conference convinced City Council to give the erosion committee permission to pursue a remedy for our erosion problem through the existing Corps mitigation framework. The local Corps office granted that it would be receptive to dropping the lawsuit and entertaining a request for a Section 1-11 review of the relationship between the CHNP and erosion on Folly.

The News and Courier

FOUNDED JAN. 10, 1803

CHARLESTON, S.C., FRIDAY, SEPTEMBER 22, 1978

Up Against Nature Once Again

Residents of Folly Beach may be within their rights in throwing their own good money after bad into another effort to hold back the Atlantic Ocean. It is other people's money, too, that it is proposed they toss away building "rip-rap" with the help of state funds, so the rest of us are entitled to hope that common sense will prevent the project from materializing.

As is frequently the case, where beach residents fly to arms against erosion, the citizens of Folly plan to counterattack the wrong place. They have been told differently many times by people in a position to know, but they persist in identifying the destruction of their beach as the product of conspiracy between wind and tide and other natural forces which they can arrest with barriers of wood and stone. They miss the point that when they tear down protective dunes they leave themselves wide open to conquest. Viewing the skeletons of previous efforts to stem the tide with the help of highway engineers and construction equipment, one would think that the futility of such an approach would speak for itself. Not at Folly Beach, however, nor in other places.

Whenever an outsider raises a dissenting voice to the claims of beach communities for assistance in rescuing them from their own mistakes, he risks being told to mind his own business. That is easily rebutted by pointing out that it is everybody's business when tax resources are called into the picture. Apart from that, however, who in the rest of South Carolina wants to stand idly by while beach communities fight futile battles against the sea? Folly and similar beach areas are not islands unto themselves. They belong to South Carolinians in general. Every day which passes on which beach residents refuse to face the facts of life concerning erosion postpones the day when really effective protective measures can be taken.

The ills which afflict Folly do not arise from local forces. For a variety of reasons, many of them beyond the control of local people, they cannot be controlled by local operations. If residents would let nature take its course, however, she would restore protections which served from time immemorial, until men came, building houses. The wasting process would be delayed. Every day that beach people lose in accepting that proposition and putting it to work for them — and us — is a victory for the sea against them, and us.

Folly had detractors on more than one front. *News and Courier,* Sept 1978.

Coastal Council rejected the conference finding that the $400,000 in state funding should be escrowed and demanded that it be spent, and soon. The erosion committee considered our options and since qualification for aid from the Corps was primarily tied to a community's value as a recreational resource, we asked to use the money to implement the alternative proposal and rebuild our missing sand dunes, improve beach access at Folly, and repair existing groins. The state gave us permission to use the money to those ends. In 1981, we repaired fourteen existing groins and, helped by local architect Dinos Liollio, we presented plans, took bids, and constructed 20 prototype walkovers, including the state's first two handicapped walkovers at 9th street West and 16th Street East. They are still in use today.

We dropped the lawsuit and negotiated with the Charleston District office of the Corps of Engineers. Thanks to the new commander, Lieutenant Colonel Bernie Stallman, we reached an agreement that they would provide funding for a preliminary review of the relationship between erosion on Folly and the navigation project under Section 1-11. City Council agreed to fund a consultant. Folly's first "scoping meeting" with the Corps occurred on February 2, 1981.

In March, the erosion committee interviewed several coastal engineers to get a feel for whom to hire as our consultant. After the interviews, there was no doubt in our minds that Eric Olsen, having recently executed a successful section 1-11 attempt, was the candidate with the most pertinent experience. City Council approved Olsen's contract for what we thought would be a two-month study, a major underestimate. A year later, City Council pulled the funding for the consultant. They simply could not comprehend how a study could take multiple years. (The total study time exceeded six years.)

The council had obviously never dealt with the Corps of Engineers, which was both frustrating and humorous. I remember a breakfast meeting at the Holiday Inn in 1986 with Thurmond Morgan, the top civilian at the Corps. I asked him why this study had taken six years and would cost over $400,000 when I understood that the study could be done by a private consultant on an Apple 2-E in six months for $60,000. "Richard," he said, "if you will remember what I have to say next, it will make all your dealings with the Corps make sense. At the Corps, overhead is our most important product." When you are dealing with the Corps, work proceeds on their schedule.

The erosion committee constantly struggled with City Council about funding. As late as the spring of 1983, petty bickering and personality politics kept me from having the funding to pay Eric for his help with the study, much to the dismay of the citizens—as expressed at several City Council meetings.

Long story short, Eric did a masterful job and thanks to our then-Congressional representatives, Tommy Hartnett and Arthur Ravenel Jr., and US Senator Ernest Hollings, we were allowed broad access to review and comment on the Corps' study conclusions before they were published. The career members of the local Corps office were still very much of the opinion that the CHNP was not the cause of our erosion problems. Frankly, a retirement or two helped us maintain traction.

Eric countered the negative and questionable findings of the Corps' research whenever necessary. When we couldn't afford to bring Eric from Jacksonville for a meeting, he coached me on how to bring our case to bear.

On many occasions, City Council threatened to stop the funding because it was taking so long. The erosion committee had to plead with City Council to let us complete the study, which, by its very nature, is complicated and arduous. Eric charged us a little more than $20,000 for the time he spent helping Folly over a six-year period. Folly should canonize him.

After six years of intensive scientific give and take and a host of meetings to negotiate differing views of the facts of the relationship between the jetties and Folly's erosion, the outcome didn't have as much to do with accumulated facts as it did with persistence. It all came to a head at a meeting in the spring of 1987 between Eric and me and the southeastern regional engineer of the U.S. Army Corps of Engineers at the Coastal Engineering Research Center in Vicksburg, Mississippi. When the meeting ended, the regional engineer said, "Listen, you think the jetties are ninety percent at fault. We think it's thirty percent. We will give you fifty-seven percent. That will trigger an eighty-five percent federal participation in the renourishment of your island for the next fifty years. We can debate it further and take five or ten more years to study it, or we can agree and proceed with putting the beach back together. What would you like to do?"

It wasn't a difficult question to answer. City Council agreed to accept the conclusion of the Corps of Engineers. The report, "The

Evaluation of the Impact of Charleston Harbor Jetties on Folly Island, South Carolina" was formally accepted by the Corps in August 1987. The Erosion Committee's nine-year effort was a success. Folly became the eighteenth example in our nation's history of a successful Section 1-11 review attributing shoreline damages to a navigation project. Our 15% match is one of the lowest local matches ever authorized.

Interestingly enough, Save the Light, Inc. incorporated the Section 1-11 cost-sharing schedule when it partnered with the local district to place a new cofferdam around the Morris Island Lighthouse in 2008. If the local Corps office of 1979 had been as enlightened as today's district office, this would have been a much shorter story.

Receiving an official commitment from the Corps and getting the project in place was as complicated as one might expect. In early 1989, the Corps told us it would take another three years to begin the process of renourishing the beach. To avoid the nagging of councilmen Benson and Linville, I convinced the district colonel to go to a City Council meeting each month to brief the council on the Corps' progress.

Our possession of a successful Section 1-11, which binds the federal government to be there for Folly for fifty years from its 1987 conclusion, played a critical role as Folly faced the potential damaging effects of the Beachfront Management Act of 1988 and Hurricane Hugo in 1989. Following Hugo, Mayor Linville used our successful Section 1-11 review to work with Senator Hollings to facilitate the on-time implementation of the 1992 Corps of Engineers' renourishment. Subsequent projects have also been able to use the 15% local cost-sharing dictated by the successful 1987 study.

Chapter 15

The 1988 Beachfront Management Bill
1985–1990

The state of the seawalls at East 5th Street, 1986.

I had been speaking publicly about the need for a statewide approach to solving South Carolina's beach erosion problems ever since I was introduced to the successes of the Florida Shore & Beach Preservation Association (FSBPA) at their annual meeting in 1978. Over the years, the FSBPA had established a coalition among Florida's coastal communities, the Jacksonville District of the U.S. Army Corps of Engineers, and the Florida Legislature to create a statewide commitment to the health of its beaches.

Until the mid-1980s, beach erosion in South Carolina was considered a problem unique to Folly Beach. As time passed, more communities experienced erosion firsthand. As the effects of erosion became more widespread, the coastal communities understood the need for cooperation.

In early 1985, Mayor Erick Ficken of Myrtle Beach, Mayor Joel Thompson of Seabrook, Mayor Michael Malanick of Hilton Head Island, Mayor Melvin Anderegg of Sullivan's Island, and I worked together to form the first chapter of the South Carolina Shore and Beach Preservation Association (SCSBPA). Like its sister in Florida, it was a nonprofit organization dedicated to fostering a state-wide approach to solving shoreline problems. We held our first organizational gathering in Myrtle Beach on January 30. Mayor Ficken and I addressed the Coastal Council on October 25 and held our second statewide gathering on Hilton Head Island on January 31, 1986. Our program included presentations by Senator James Waddell, Legislative Chair of the South Carolina Coastal Council; Dr. Robert Dean of the University of Florida; Dr. Robert Pomeroy of Clemson University; and Dr. Margaret Davidson of the Sea Grant consortium.

This organization proved to be an important way to coordinate coastal community cooperation when, in response to a gathering storm of coastal problems, the state government took legislative action.

In October 1986, I was asked by Senator James Waddell to be a member of Governor Richard Riley's Blue-Ribbon Panel on Beachfront Management. The grand scheme was to gather as many stakeholders with as divergent interests as possible and for those stakeholders to arrive at a statewide approach to deal with the coastal erosion. We were tasked with creating a unified policy statement and presenting a legislative framework to the South Carolina Legislature. The Legislature would then create a beachfront management law to guide the state's approach to managing its beaches for the next forty years. The panel was chaired by Mayor Ficken and was convened by Coastal Council in Columbia.

Formed in the late-1970s, Coastal Council was a semi-autonomous, quasi-legislative body tasked with regulating activity in South Carolina's coastal zone. When the Blue-Ribbon Panel met in 1986, Coastal Council was chaired by Dr. Wayne Beam and its legislative chair was State Senator James Waddell of Beaufort.

From the panel's earliest meetings, there were indications that the committee would embrace a one-size-fits-all conclusion that would result in a retreat from the coast. A baseline would be established and, as erosion progressed beyond that baseline, structures and infrastructure damaged by the encroaching ocean would no longer be protected and would have to be removed.

For Folly, that meant that no new seawalls would be allowed and if one of the existing seawalls was damaged, it could not be repaired. The structure behind the damaged seawall would be fully exposed to the encroaching ocean and be lost. Folly's erosion rate at this point was about six feet a year. Given that erosion rate, Folly's very existence depended completely on keeping her seawalls intact.

I joined a minority contingent of similarly affected communities who tried in vain to persuade the committee that there were large parts of South Carolina's developed shoreline that would be severely harmed by a retreat approach. We proposed that if the law was going to be successful and fair, there had to be a renourishment component. Further, we argued that South Carolina would have to tweak the overall approach to be community specific. Our proposals gained no traction.

Folly's beach was in the worst shape of all other state beaches, so it was even more important that the state not adopt a fall back/fall in, or abandon the coast approach. By the time I was put on the panel, our Section 1-11 review was complete and the causal relationship between the jetties and Folly's erosion was a proven fact. As mayor of the most vulnerable and least powerful coastal community, I faced the possibility that, to be true to my community, I would have to vote against the findings of the Blue-Ribbon Panel. I was likely to be the only member to do so.

I expressed those concerns to Mayor Ficken, the panel chairman. Shortly afterward, I was asked by former Governor Dr. James Edwards to meet at the Med Deli in South Windemere for lunch. Dr. Edwards asked me not to vote against the proposal because it was important that the vote be unanimous. I told him that the bill would be the kiss of death for my community because some 200 buildings would be prohibited from rebuilding if damaged in a storm. I also reminded him that Folly's erosion was not a natural event and we were being punished for a problem we did not create. I told him I would have to vote against the panel's conclusions unless the committee could somehow find a way for my community to be exempted from the seawall and set back provisions.

Dr. Edwards and I agreed, in principle, that Folly should be exempted from enforcement of the seawall and setback provisions of the bill because our successful Corps of Engineers Section 1-11 study proved that Folly's erosion was not a natural occurrence.

I was assured that if I voted for the bill as it existed, he would help to carve out that exemption in the bill as an amendment in the legislative approval process. I knew him and trusted him. I consulted with City Council and they supported me. I voted in favor, and the conclusions of the panel passed unanimously.

The Blue-Ribbon panel presented its findings to the Legislature in January 1987, but the panel's conclusion to retreat from the coast drew such heavy criticism that a bill was not passed until the end of the 1988 legislative session. As we had predicted, the biggest problem was that the legislation proposed a setback line and declared that any structure lost that was behind the line could not be rebuilt, an approach that opened the legal can of worms of whether the state could legislatively take a person's property through regulation without compensation. Under the new law, a lot of expensive beachfront property was at risk. People up and down the coast were understandably upset. Thanks to all the confusion and conflict, the remedy promised to Folly did not come as easily as Governor Edwards indicated it would. June 1988 found me still battling to have the promises made at the Med Deli realized. In March 1989, the *News and Courier* referred to our effort as "threatening to return South Carolina to the dark ages of reckless coastal development."

The retreat policy proposed penalties but offered no assistance. As the minority of the panel had predicted, the all-stick-and-no-carrot approach was a hard sell. Other coastal communities such as Hilton Head Island, Fripp Island, Edisto Island, Pawley's Island, Sunset Beach, Cherry Grove, and Garden City wanted modifications or exemptions. It was maddeningly difficult to get legislators to understand the difference between Folly's unique position and all the other requests for leniency.

In February 1988, I appeared before the State Environmental Affairs Subcommittee, which was reviewing the working draft of the beachfront management legislation. I asked, to no avail, for a more balanced or community-by-community approach to beachfront management. Mayor Ficken and I later appeared on behalf of the SCSBPA to lobby for a renourishment funding component to the bill but got only a tepid response.

After the 1988 Legislative Session, I learned that Folly's freedom from the potentially disastrous effects of the bill would come with an unexpected price. I was presenting our case for an exemption to the Charleston County Legislative Delegation at a meeting on Folly when I was asked by the chairman, "If you had to choose between getting the exemption or never seeking aid from the state in funding renourishment, which one would you choose?" I was really on the spot and answered, "I don't understand the logic of the choice, but if I were forced to make the choice, I would choose the latter." My answer became reality.

The state legislature forced Folly to make that very decision. On June 21, City Council accepted those terms, hoping, as the demands on the state for action on renourishment and the value of tourism dollars became more apparent, that the wisdom of including Folly in renourishment funding would be acknowledged.

In a letter dated June 23, 1988, I wrote Senator John C. Hayes III, the new legislative chair of Coastal Council, and formally requested that Folly Beach be exempted from the seawall provisions of the Breach Front Management Bill, accepting that funding stipulation. In July, I got notice from the Corps that the Beachfront Management Bill could jeopardize our relationship with the Corps. If the bill caused property values to drop below a certain level, the cost/benefit analysis done by the Corps might not be valid anymore, and our renourishment project could be disqualified. Thanks to Senator Hollings, it did not come to that.

The Beachfront Management Law (Act 634 of 1988), a modification of Act 123 of 1977, passed in June of 1988. Section 48-39-300 dealt with erosion control structures. Though the language of Folly's exemption had been agreed upon in principle, the promised exemption was not in the 1988 iteration of the bill. Though SC Representative Robert Barber and SC Senator Sherry Martschink worked hard over the next year to include Folly in state renourishment funding, it never happened. The attitude of the Legislature seemed to be that Folly's asking for exemption was an insult!

Although the effort to gain an exemption was pronounced dead on arrival by *The News and Courier* in April 1989, the SC Senate passed an exemption for Folly, tying our erosion to the Charleston Harbor jetties through our Corps of Engineers Section 1-11 study. On May 10, the Senate bill died in the SC House, and we were back in limbo.

As usual, *The News and Courier* was no help. In a July 13, 1988 editorial titled "How Much a Victim?" The editorial stated, "It is likely true that the jetties contribute to erosion at Folly, but it is indisputably true that those same jetties contribute to the prosperity of the area of which Folly Beach is a part. Balancing out those truths, what is left? Nothing, we would say, that justifies Folly as deserving special exemptions from the Beach Front Management Act."

Say what? It seemed to me that *The News and Courier* would have had us play the role of the sacrificial lamb. I could never understand why.

The News and Courier

ARTHUR M. WILCOX, Editor
ROBERT J. COX, Assistant Editor

Founded Jan. 10, 1803

R. L. SCHREADLEY, Associate Editor
MICHAEL J. BONAFIELD, Associate Editor

CHARLESTON, S.C. WEDNESDAY, JANUARY 11, 1989, PAGE 6-A

Folly Beach's erosion problem

Rallying to the cause of Folly residents whose beach keeps washing away, Sen. Sherry Martschink has repeated once again the oft-repeated allegation that the federal government has wronged her constituents by building the Charleston Harbor jetties. Mrs. Martschink, like everybody else, knows the sequence of events involving Folly Beach and those jetties, but we'll mention it anyway: First came the jetties; then came Folly Beach; then (long afterwards) came those residents of Folly Beach who now claim to be wronged.

So wherein lies the claim that the government has created problems for them by building jetties? One could argue just as easily, and more accurately, that while there might not be any erosion problems at Folly if there weren't any jetties, there certainly wouldn't be any problem if there weren't any people to complain about it.

The provisions of the state's Beachfront Management Act are irrelevant to the question of who has caused the problems at Folly. It won't change a thing for better or worse that has been done there. It could, on the other hand, prevent more problems of the same kind.

Folly residents (and Sen. Martschink) are wrong twice over as they go about trying to solve Folly's problem. Wrong to blame it all on other people. Wrong again to try to undermine the Beachfront Management Act, a law which can protect them from their own mistakes in the future.

A *News and Courier* editorial discounting our request for
an exemption from the 1988 Beachfront Management Act.

As the 1989 legislative session began, there was still no consensus that Folly was likely to get an exemption from the seawall and set back provisions of the bill. A January editorial in *The News and Courier* was solidly against any special provision for Folly.

In August 1989, the state put $10 million in the state budget for renourishment projects. Folly applied for funds. Lawyers for Coastal Council ruled that Folly was ineligible for any of that funding because of our agreement to the terms of our exemption from seawall restrictions (still unrealized) in the 1988 law. Maddening!

The Folly community was active in trying to get legislators to understand the special circumstances at Folly and Senator Martschink never tired of making our case.

The Beachfront Management Act was revisited in 1990 and substantially amended by Act 607. This time, language exempting Folly from the seawall provisions was included in section 48-39-300:

A local governing body, if it notifies the council before July 1, 1990, may exempt from the provisions of Section 48-39-290, relating to reconstruction and removal of erosion control devices, the shorelines fronting the Atlantic Ocean under its jurisdiction where coastal erosion has been shown to be attributed to a federally authorized navigation project as documented by the findings of a Section 111 Study conducted under the authority of the Rivers and Harbors Act of 1968, as amended by the Water Resources Development Act of 1986 and approved by the United States Army Corps of Engineers. Erosion control devices exempt under this section must not be constructed seaward of their existing location, increased in dimension, or rebuilt out of materials different from that of the original structure.

Finally, Act 181 of 1993 amended the language of section 48-39-300 again to reflect the restructuring of Coastal Council to become the Office of Coastal Resource Management (OCRM) and come under the umbrella of the South Carolina Department of Health and Environmental Control (DHEC). The word "department" was substituted for the word "council" in the first line.

In April 1989, I prevailed upon the Charleston County Council to establish a Charleston County Committee to Restore Folly Beach and to populate it with a host of people dedicated to renourishing the beach. That was just one month before my resignation.

Chapter 16

Final Straws

The years 1988 and 1989 were tough for me. Bob Linville and Penny Travis were elected to Council in 1988 and Wallace Benson took his seat in early 1989. As I said before, with their inclusion, the council became a contentious arena again. As my daddy used to say, "Enough is a-plenty." For the decorum of our meetings to sink back to the disrespectful level of polemics of the past frankly broke my heart and was sucking the life out of me.

I was fighting to get the promises of our exemption from the seawall section of the 1988 Beachfront Management Law honored, keep from losing the support of the Army Corps of Engineers, manage my dental practice, be present in my marriage, deal with Bob and Wallace's antagonism, and stomach a partisan attack about my salary when a new controversy muscled its way to center stage—based on Frank and Lee Roeber's attempt to build a 270-boat dry stack marina on the property that eventually became the Charleston County boat landing on Folly.

Frank and Lee, my friends and neighbors, had been ardent FIRA supporters and a critical part of our successful effort to prevent tall buildings and down-zoning of the island. I enjoyed their company—we often got together for cocktails at each other's homes to discuss the politics of the day. I considered them political allies.

They purchased Camper's Cove, a recreational vehicle camping site next to the existing public landing in 1983, revamped it, and renamed it Pelican Cove Riverview Resort. The business seemed to do well. There was a small public boat ramp between the eastern edge of their property and the Folly River bridge.

After operating the campground for four years, they decided to change the use of the property to a 270-boat dry-stack marina. They presented plans to the Planning and Zoning Board of March 1987 and won approval. The following month, City Council reversed the board's decision.

In August 1987, the Roebers asked for a permit directly from the building inspector. I spoke with Frank and Lee and said that I would oppose their project. It was a tense conversation, somewhat softened by the fact that they were confident that they would prevail. The vote on City Council was divided, but the majority supported me. I had three objections.

First, I felt the Roebers' proposal did not comply with Folly's zoning ordinance, which had a clearly reasoned and defined marine commercial district (C-3) on the west end of the island where Sunset Cay Marina is now. When I moved to Folly in 1975, a marina/shrimp dock run by the Thompson family was there. By 1987, Danny O'Rourk had purchased the Thompson property and was making improvements to the area. We clearly had a functional marine commercial district.

Folly's 1977 land-use plan was sensitive to the need to limit the location of marine commercial stating, "Only one part of the island lends itself to these type operations: an area on the west end which was previously used for such operations. It is obvious that marine commercial activity be confined to a well-defined area because of the pollution problems that always accompany the repair and storage of boats." Both Coastal Council and the city were opposed to the project because the pollution associated with it would demand that the only oyster grounds accessible by foot in Charleston County would have to be closed.

Second, I could not envision a worse sight for people coming onto the island: a 280-feet long and 40-feet tall tin box.

Third, I was concerned that congestion at the adjacent boat ramp would be compounded because their plans indicated that they would not have enough parking spaces for their business. Charleston's traffic planner, Howard Chapman, agreed about the inadequacy of parking and opposed the project in testimony before Coastal Council.

I advised Ed Wilder, the building inspector, to turn down the permit application because it violated the zoning ordinance as supported by City Council. He did. The Roebers sued, arguing that the current zoning, C-1, was a broad category that allowed the business they proposed.

Their Coastal Council permit was denied but granted on appeal. Folly appealed the permit to the courts. I was shocked and disappointed that Coastal Council would presume to give a permit in what was essentially a zoning dispute between Folly and two citizens. The Coastal Council permit didn't help our case and we lost in the lower court. Judge Condon ruled in the Roebers' favor on January 27, 1988. In February, City Council voted 4-2 to appeal. Tommy Bolus and Wayne Hembree voted against appealing because they thought that Judge Condon's ruling was so thorough that spending money on an appeal was foolish. In May, FIRA donated $1,200 toward the cost of the appeal.

Several months after Councilman Wayne Hembree was reelected in the spring of 1988, he moved from Folly to take a new job and gave up his council seat. Until an election could be held, City Council was reduced to six members. Bob Linville requested another council vote about whether to continue to appeal the lower court's decision. It failed, three to three, so I asked City Council to seek guidance by holding a non-binding referendum. On May 18, the referendum showed just how deeply the community was divided. By a vote of 373-300, the referendum favored continuing the appeal to the South Carolina Supreme Court.

On August 31, 1988, the Roebers offered City Council $25,000 to drop its appeal in an open City Council meeting. That meeting was the closest I ever got to losing control of the room. Bob Linville moved to accept the money, which was supported by Penny Travis and Tommy Bolus. Rex Whitcomb, Marianne Read, and I voted against the motion (3-3). The motion failed. The audience was offended by what they considered an effort by the Roebers to bribe City Council. Once the accusations and recriminations got a head of steam, I was all but helpless to get the room to settle. Secretly, I was happy that by going public, the Roebers had riled up opposition to the project. The vote meant that the case would go on to the Supreme Court.

Whether to continue the court fight against the dry stack became an issue again in the election to fill Wayne's seat. As you may recall from Chapter 13, the November 1988 election was a protracted mess that resulted in a City Council seat being vacant for five months. The city did not know whether Wallace Benson or Rogers Oglesby would be seated, a question not resolved until April 1989.

During the vacancy there were questions about the fate of the appeal. Wallace Benson was against continuing the suit because of cost, and Rogers Oglesby wanted to pursue it. Thankfully, a consensus developed that whoever was seated, the city would let the appeal continue. Ben Peeples and I were arguing in the city's defense when my life changed.

Breaking point

Whether big government or small, elected officials in the midst of weathering a controversial stand rely on an inner circle of people for political support and friendship. I had regular meetings with friends that opposed the dry-stack marina. Keeping the appeal in play had proven to be a delicate balancing act and I needed all the comfort and support I could get.

On May 10, 1989, I got a call from Jack Hall. He and his wife Betty and Dee and Oscar Oakes, then chairman of FIRA, were four of my most crucial supporters regarding the dry-stack question. I met with them often as a part of a group that included other citizens. Jack asked whether I could meet the group after work.

When I arrived, only Jack, Betty, Oscar, and Dee were there. The usual conviviality was missing. I should have figured that the evening would not go well when I wasn't offered a cocktail. Pleasantries were exchanged, and then Jack said, "Richard, I'm afraid we've got some bad news for you."

"Really? What kind of bad news?"

"Well, I guess there's no reason to beat around the bush. Oscar, Dee, Betty, and I have decided that we are going to support the dry stack."

"You can't be serious! We've met a dozen times to talk about this. We've worked together on keeping the votes on Council in place. We've agreed that this is the worst possible business to have as the front door of the community. This makes no sense. What happened?"

Oscar chimed in. "Richard, you know that I own the two buildings next door to the campground and have been using them in my business. I've decided that having the dry stack there will make my property more valuable."

I was stunned. "More valuable? How would it make them more valuable?"

"We're thinking there will be some supportive businesses that might need a place to locate on Folly, and we want to be able to rent them out."

"What about your chairmanship of FIRA? How's that going to work? The organization has openly supported my position and has even given money to help defend against the Roeber's lawsuit."

"Yeah, I know—it's uncomfortable. I guess I need to resign."

"Yes, I would think so."

I turned to Jack. "And you and Betty? What's your story?"

"Well, Betty is planning to run for the council and she's afraid that if we are against the dry stack, it will hurt her chances for election. We think that the political tide has turned and that she just needs to be quiet about this for now."

"After all we've been through together?" I stopped to gather my thoughts. "There's got to be more to this than what you are telling me. No one does an about-face like this without thinking about it a long time. We just met in full agreement last week. How could this happen in a week? This really sucks!"

Betty held up one hand. "Now don't get excited, Richard. We still want to be friends."

"I'm not excited—I'm dumbfounded! I'm sad and I feel betrayed. And let me be clear about something. Friends don't lead friends down the path of cooperation and then cut them off at the knees. I am going to go now before I say something I might regret." I turned walked out of the room.

On the way home, I pulled over and parked at the washout. I looked out on the moonlit ocean with a thousand-yard stare and, as I tried to come to grips with the loss of the support of my friends, I was overcome by a deep sense of hopelessness. When their betrayal was added to the accumulated stress of the constant controversy of my time in office, something in me snapped.

The tension that accompanied my position had been weighing heavily on my mind for some time. I had been in office for over 11 years, and it seemed that I had spent most of that time fighting against what others considered progress. Given the additional contentiousness that adding Bob Linville and Wallace Benson brought to the council, it was clear that the level of tension would only get worse.

I remembered an incident from the previous February. At the time, Larry Ridgeway and I vacationed in the Florida Keys twice a year. He would drive from Florence on I-95 and I would meet him in Hardeeville. With the permission of the mayor of Hardeeville, I'd leave my car at the police station. On the way back from that trip to Florida, I stopped to pick up my car and went inside the police station to thank them for watching out for it—and to thank the mayor for once again giving me permission to leave it with them. "I guess you haven't heard," said the dispatcher. "The mayor died since you dropped your car off. He had a heart attack."

Of course, I hadn't heard, and I said I was very sorry to hear about his passing. Then out of the back of the station came a disembodied voice. "Aw, that old son of a bitch? I'm glad he's gone. All he ever did was screw with people's plans and get in the way of progress."

I had not been able to get that voice out of my head. I suspected that my opponents would have a similar response if I suddenly died. I couldn't bear the thought that they might get a similar chance to rejoice—just two weeks earlier, I'd been sitting at my desk talking to my lab technician on the phone when the room started spinning and I'd fallen to the floor. I lost consciousness and was hospitalized. Three days of tests were inconclusive, but the doctors surmised I had had a stress-induced transient ischemic attack (TIA)—a mini stroke.

Like the proverbial straw that broke the camel's back, losing my friends' support—combined with the stress of having been the public face of controversy for so long—caused my mind to rebel.

When I got home, I sat down with my wife and told her what had happened. Nancy had never been a fan of my being in office in the first place—she resented the time and attention that my service required and wasn't the least bit subtle in expressing her frustration. My dental practice was growing rapidly despite my best efforts to run it on hold, and it had become increasingly difficult for me to fulfill my obligations on all fronts. If I got home before 10 p.m. on a weeknight, it was because I had forgotten a meeting. I often woke up in the morning on the couch— in a suit.

Nancy listened quietly. Then, knowing what the stress of my having both a profession and an elected position was costing our marriage, she gave me an ultimatum—either I resigned and devoted my energies to my family and business or she would leave. I believe she said, "If you aren't going to be leaving office, then I am going to be leaving you."

We had had similar discussions before and I had always argued that I had no choice but to complete my term. But this time, I looked her and said, "You know, you're right. I can't go on."

I met with Ben Peeples that night. We talked about all that we had been through and all that had been accomplished. He said, "Richard, my friend, you have to do what is best for you. I think you've earned the right to put yourself and all the people that depend on you first. I will draft a letter of resignation for your signature."

My resignation was announced the following morning and a wave of peace washed over me. That peace, unfortunately, would be short-lived.

Chapter 17

It's Not Over Till It's Over

I had just been elected mayor for the first time when I went into Centerville Laundry to drop off some shirts. The girl behind the counter was a young black lady I had come to know. She spoke in the Gullah-Geechee dialect that used to be so common in Charleston.

"Dr. Beck," she said, "I guess you woan be dune no mo denistry no mo now dat you da mayor."

I laughed. "No, Lucy—being the mayor is not for the money. My salary is only $100 a month."

She paused and then cocked her head to the side and squinched up her face. "No-o-o-o! A hundre dolla a munt fo a headache evy day?"

It's the best description of local politics I have ever heard.

Old wounds re-opened

In 1986, at the beginning of my second term as mayor, I asked City Council in open session to give me a raise. My salary as mayor during my first term was, as I said above, $100 per month. The city attorney noted that the state salary law had been amended in 1979 (5-7-170) and had removed the mayor from the stipulations that govern when a raise can take effect. City Council amended our local ordinance to match the state ordinance and raised my salary to $400 per month.

Shortly after the raise was given, political opponents characterized the raise as unethical and filed a complaint with the then-State Ethics Commission Chairman Charlie Condon, who said that the raise probably should not have gone into effect until the start of my next term, but that the raise was *not* unethical because it was done openly—with the approval of the city's attorney and the blessing of state law.

By 1989, both Bob Linville and Wallace Benson had gained a seat on the City Council, providing fertile ground for two citizens to reintroduce the question of the legitimacy of my 1986 raise. Those two citizens secured an opinion from the state Attorney General (AG) Travis Medlock's office that the raise had violated state law.

Charlie Condon, by then the Ninth Circuit Solicitor, countered, saying that given the way the law was written, "The AG's take could be an honest difference in legal opinion between the AG's office and Folly Beach City Attorney Ben Peeples." He noted that aggrieved citizens could sue if they were unhappy. The threat to sue was made.

Shortly after that, Peeples reminded the audience at a City Council meeting that I could not be sued successfully since I never voted for anything. On April 18, 1989, a month before my resignation, Bob Linville introduced a motion that would have forced me to return the money he claimed I had been unlawfully paid. The motion demanding that I return my salary failed on a Linville, Benson, Travis/Bolus, Whitcomb, Read split, a 3-3 vote with my abstention.

Without knowing I would resign, the two citizen opponents had chosen the very first council meeting following my resignation (May 17) to challenge the council to either take the money back from me or face court action. This time, the Linville-authored resolution got Tommy Bolus's support and passed 4-3. Two weeks later, that motion proved itself hypocritical when City Council unanimously refused to change the language of the law that had allowed me to gain the raise back in 1986.

On June 7, a month after my resignation, City Council put the question of when a salary increase for the mayor could go into effect to rest. *The News and Courier* put it this way: "Although Folly Beach City Council has asked former mayor Richard Beck to repay $6,300 from a controversial 1986 pay hike, Council Tuesday night failed to repair the law that allowed Beck to receive the raise in the first place." Council refused to add the mayor back to an ordinance that would limit raises to the beginning of the following term.

Bob Linville, who was now running for mayor said, "I don't see why we are changing it [the law] for the sake of changing it. If it [Richard's raise] was perfectly legal two years ago, has something occurred that makes it illegal now?" Running for mayor had apparently caused Bob to lose his passion for ruminative righteousness. He voted against re-including the mayor's position into the ordinance. The two citizens sued but nothing ever came of it. The journey was finally over.

The News and Courier published a favorable editorial praising my service and my role as their adversary. The paper and I had been in almost constant disagreement over the condescending and punitive attitude it expressed when covering the news from Folly. The paper expressed a grudging respect for the way I defended Folly. In addition, it bemoaned the petty and malicious controversy regarding my pay raise. I received many cards and letters thanking me for my service. When I reread them, I wept.

Rex Whitcomb was mayor pro tempore and took over my duties at a time of great professional stress. Recently, he told me that he has never quite forgiven me for passing that baton to him at that particular point in time.

By September, Bob Linville was elected mayor and then early on the morning of Friday, September 21, 1989, Hurricane Hugo hit Charleston County. My having resigned in May turned out to be one of the best examples of good timing in my life.

Bob did an excellent job of commanding forces during Folly's recovery from Hugo. Helped by Senator Hollings, he got Folly's first Corps of Engineers-assisted installment of beach renourishment, promised under the successful Section 1-11, completed by its original 1992 projected date.

Between my conversation with the Halls and the Oakes the night of my resignation and the arrival of Hurricane Hugo, Betty Hall challenged Bob Linville for the position of mayor and lost. The city's court case against the dry stack marina permit continued.

On Thursday, September 20, 1989, one day before Hugo hit, Ben Peeples was arguing the case of *Roeber v. City of Folly Beach* before the SC Supreme Court. If not Hugo, he said, then the son of Hugo would one day come along and flatten the structure to everyone's detriment. The Roebers' attorney, Gedney Howe III, argued that dry stack structures were built so well that they could survive anything that Mother Nature might throw at them.

When Hugo hit early the next morning, every dry-stack marina in its path became a hopeless jumble of timber, sheets of tin roofing, and broken boats. The Roebers abandoned their effort to build the marina and when the Charleston County Parks and Recreation Commission later approached them about buying the property to build a public boat landing, they sold it. Lee Roeber served on the PRC Board of Directors and Frank, Lee, and I later rekindled our friendship.

Once again, the value of delay had proven its worth. Events unfolded so that we now have an excellent public boat landing instead of a dry-stack marina as the gateway to Folly.

Chapter 18

Reflections

Ilook back on my time in office with pride and often wish that everyone who calls Folly home today could have had the chance to live here in those turbulent, passionate, idyllic times. I wish that everyone had the memories I have of what Folly was like when I moved there in 1975.

As mayor, I was privileged to be part of a group of dedicated citizens who changed the destiny of the community. Together, we accomplished a great deal:

- The area behind the seawall at the end of Center Street is the heart of the commercial district and was falling apart. We stabilized the area and rehabilitated the seawall, which provided the platform on which to build a vital business community.

- The availability of sewer was critical to the long-term health of the business district, and we brought it to the island while also protecting the community from runaway commercial expansion by attaching the limitation that it could not be expanded without the express permission of the community in a binding referendum.

- We proved that the Charleston Harbor jetties were the proximate cause of Folly's erosion problems. The successful effort guarantees a fifty-year commitment by the federal government to an eighty-five percent federal and fifteen percent local cost-sharing arrangement on future renourishment projects through the year 2037.

- Thanks to the vision of Rogers Oglesby and the hard work of FIRA, we downzoned everything outside of the commercial district to single family zoning, including the fifty-seven-acre Seabrook tract, which was slated for a large commercial development. FIRA was also the movement that forced City Council to set reasonable height limits in the commercial and residential districts. Those height limits prevented the development of no fewer than 400 multi-family living units by defeating three different large-scale, high-rise projects. The defeat of a six-story condominium project to the immediate east of the Holiday Inn (now the Tides) allowed the county fishing pier to become a reality.

- In 1981, we prevented the development of multi-family structures on the western tip of the Island and made the PRC beach park a reality. We went to court to prevent a dry stack marina from being the gateway structure for Folly. Our efforts paved the way for the development of the public boat landing enjoyed by so many people.

- Finally, we were the only beach community to obtain an exemption from the seawall and set-back provisions of the 1988 Beachfront Management law, which allowed our front beach property owners to protect their properties when so many of them were vulnerable.

Against sometimes overwhelming odds, we laid the groundwork for Folly to develop as a spirited, family-oriented, low-density, low-rise community, focused more on the quality of life than on development and tourism.

Chapter 19
Déjà Vu All Over Again
2023

In 1986, with a sympathetic City Council in place, I attempted to get Folly to develop a 20-year planning approach called an island plan. Unlike a conventional land use ordinance, an island plan takes into consideration the limitations placed on the island by environmental and quality-of-life issues in developing an optimum population for the island.

In my research, I discovered that this method had been successfully used on Sanibel Island, Florida, and I wanted us to duplicate their approach to planning the future. Margaret Davidson helped me secure a grant, and the city held some nineteen public hearings. In the end, I couldn't get the community or City Council to embrace long-term planning of that level of complexity.

Given the problems that Folly is having in 2023 with the commercialization that investor-owned short-term rentals (ISTRs) bring to the residential areas, I wish that island plan had been implemented. It would be helpful today if the concept of optimum population had become part of the government's lexicon 37 years ago.

As I sit here today, I am struck by the irony of the fact that I have delayed the publishing of this work for four months because the question of how much of our residential community will be commercialized is at the heart of a *third* use of the initiative and referendum portion of the Home Rule Act in Folly's history.

Once again, a citizens group is pitted against commercial interests and a hostile City Council majority in a struggle to preserve the residential integrity of the island. It's 1984 all over again.

Folly's housing stock has always been a mixture of permanent residences and part-time residences and both have always been involved in rentals. Up until, say, 2010, Folly's housing stock was used in four ways. Some homes were second homes and their owners either rented their houses as weekly rentals while they were away or didn't rent them at all. Other owners never visited and used the homes as long-term rental opportunities. Permanent residents occupied the rest of the homes. There were some short-term rentals that were less than a week—but very few. People who came to Folly for vacation were, for the most part, "regulars" who rented the same houses repetitively. We were a community of residents with some rentals.

Starting about 2010, City Council began receiving complaints about people in short-term rentals disturbing the peace in the residential districts. During the late 2010s, short-term rentals began to seriously affect the quality of life on Folly. Unfortunately, multiple City Councils pushed this problem around their plates and failed to do anything substantive to protect the permanent residents from the challenge that threatened the quiet use of their homes.

In 2020, everything changed. The COVID virus hit the United States as a part of a worldwide epidemic and within a year, 385,000 people were dead and hospitals were pushed to their very limits. Because the virus was so infectious, some form of isolation became the norm and, for two years, there seemed to be no end in sight.

People across the nation reordered their priorities. Visiting the ocean and having access to the open spaces and clean air became a nationwide obsession. More and more workers found that since they were working remotely, they could work from anywhere, preferably the beach.

Charleston had been designated as the top tourist destination in the country and/or world for the previous ten years and our area was inundated with virus refugees. The nascent online short-term rental market exploded, and so did the number of out-of-state investors wanting to capitalize on the trend.

The nature of the rental market on Folly changed—almost overnight. Folly faced an intra-national onslaught of visitors and absentee investors with no historical connections or interest in the local community. We became a mecca for disruptive visitors. Problems with noise, parking congestion and demand for services made living a quiet life on Folly increasingly difficult. People turned to City Council for solutions, but the majority of our city council, it turned out, wasn't the least bit interested in limiting the commercialization of the residential districts.

The deterioration in the quality of life grew too large to ignore. Mr. John McFarland took the initiative to form Save Folly's Future (SFF) when it was clear that the City Council was not taking the problem of livability seriously. John's  organization attracted a significant number of residents who, like him, demanded that the council do something to stop the decline in quality of life experienced by Folly's permanent residents. Under pressure from SFF, the mayor and council created an ad hoc Short-Term Rental (STR) Committee in April of 2021. This committee was tasked with studying the problem and offering possible solutions. They reported their findings and recommendations in April of 2022.

John McFarland, founder of Save Folly's Future

Three months later, on June 28, Mayor Goodwin presented City Council with an ordinance that, among other important things, capped the number of ISTRs at 800 (1/3 of the dwellings units). He said, "If you want to keep Folly residential, you are going to like my plan. If you want to see Folly fully commercialized, you are going to hate it."

City Council's majority gave an immediate answer to his rhetorical statement. The motion to adopt the plan was made by Mayor Goodwin and seconded by councilwoman Dr. Katherine Houghton. Councilman William Farley moved to table the motion, which ended all debate. Then, one by one, D.J. Rich, Adam Barker, Eddie Ellis, Billy Grooms, and William Farley voted to kill debate.

It took exactly 127 seconds for the majority of City Council to make it vividly clear that they did not support and would not allow debate on any motion that limited the commercialization of the residential district. City Council took the position that the problems could be handled by citizens and newly-hired enforcement officers.

It's a shame that City Council refused to do the work necessary to reconcile the complicated issues that surround limiting ISTRs. The council has the power to manipulate zoning and anything else it needs to produce the most equitable solution possible. By failing to give the matter the consideration it deserved, they forced citizens to protect themselves. Unfortunately, citizens had (and still have) only two options and they are not subtle ones. They can either limit the number of licenses or not. The citizens chose the former, leaving all of the complicated questions that surround this issue unresolved, perpetuating the division of the community. It forced the citizens into two camps.

Money had spoken. The number of ISTR licenses immediately shot up to 1,150 (47% of the housing stock). As baseball's Yogi Berra famously quipped, it was "déjà vu all over again." Just as Rogers Oglesby had done in 1984, John McFarland decided to put the question of limiting ISTRs into the hands of the residents of the island, and used the initiative and referendum section of the Home Rule Act (05-17-10) to create an ordinance that would amend the business license ordinance to match the mayor's ISTR limit proposal. He single-handedly began a petition drive the next day. McFarland sat day after day in a tent across from the post office, in fair weather and foul, collecting signatures and calmly explaining the benefits of limiting ISTRs to anyone who would listen.

Another important group rose to become the voice of the Folly Beach community. The Folly Beach Residents Association (FRA) was born in early 2022 from a group of full-time Folly dwellers of all stripes who came together to make a difference in their beloved community. Their mission was to partner with the city to

FOLLY BEACH
RESIDENTS ASSOCIATION

manage island life, as investors took over their neighborhoods, and then claimed to be the heart and soul of Folly. Led by Ann Peets and Kristen Kappel, FRA built a multi-pronged winning marketing and communications strategy that engaged residents through mailers, social media, emails, newspaper ads, targeted media interviews, and door-to-door discussions. The strategy successfully exposed the dark money forces at work behind the scenes and built an engaged community network of hundreds.

In order to support the proposed ordinance, SFF had to get the signatures of 15% of the number of registered voters at the last election. That number was 370. Thanks to John's dogged determination, personal financial sacrifice, and the support of FRA, SFF turned in a petition with 469 signatures to the city clerk at City Council's October 11, 2022 meeting. John asked City Council to move the question of limiting ISTRs directly to a binding referendum as soon as the signatures could be verified and an election scheduled. Mayor Goodwin asked for a 6-month moratorium on the issuance of any additional nonresident short-term rental (ISTR) licenses, but could get only three months from Council. The date for the referendum was eventually set for February 7, 2023.

As soon as it was clear that the SFF petition had a chance of success, the realtors and investors created an opposition organization called Folly United (FU) and began a program of disinformation in an attempt

to frighten voters into voting against limiting ISTRs. Our islanders were mystified, then horrified, as the FU group mounted a level of propaganda intensity and financial investment that is usually reserved to create chaos in an important election to a public office.

Dueling websites developed and the fight for the heart and soul of Folly began in earnest. As the contest between FU and SFF/ FRA heated up, it became clear that the contest was not about a community deciding its future from within as other referenda-resolved controversies on Folly had been. *This* contest was being influenced by a *national* real estate PAC called RPAC, who, backed by local realtors, wanted to make an example of "the mayor and a group of Folly residents" who "will not let this go."

At the January 18, 2023 Charleston Trident Real Estate Association's (CTAR) meeting, Josh Dix, CTAR's director of government affairs, explained, "This isn't an isolated incident on Folly. All of our municipalities are looking at Folly and if Folly can do it, the rest of them can do it." In other words, Folly, it seems, is a *test case* for RPAC.

Dix went on to outline RPAC's plans for at least four other communities in our area in 2023. A "wrecking ball that stands between restrictive councils and your right to develop your property" was the description used to describe RPAC's mission. Will Riley, CEO of CTAR, claimed that RPAC spent $56 million dollars in the US in the last election cycle alone, helping pro-real estate candidates get elected, and reported they "elect nearly 85% of our endorsed candidates to office." Josh Dix even visited Center Street to make a video supporting FU.

Scan this QR code, provided by Ann Peets and FRA, to watch an edited portion of the January CTAR meeting that specifically concerns Folly and four of its neighbors.

On February 7, 2023, despite the full court press by these powerful interests, Folly Islanders voted to implement a cap on ISTRs. The final count: 656 favoring the cap and 579 against.

The struggle on Folly is far from over and is quite likely to last another year or more. RPAC is not going to stop fighting local control of ISTRs. As I write this sentence, the SC General Assembly is considering House Bill #3253, which would penalize any community that limits ISTRs by taking away state funding and would require that ISTRs be taxed at the lower owner-occupied rate rather than the current commercial rate. Of course, this bill is supported by RPAC. If this bill becomes law, it will transform our communities into real estate profit centers.

Our city is being sued in an attempt to nullify the referendum. In *Folly East Indian Co., L.L.C. v. City of Folly Beach*, the plaintiff asserts that the cap on STR licenses is essentially a zoning change and, as such, unlawfully usurps the City Council's exclusive ability to rezone through normal statutory procedures. As Rogers Oglesby and FIRA did in 1984, John McFarland and SFF's attorney Robert Turkewitz have obtained standing in the lawsuit because it is possible that City Council will instruct the city attorney not to defend the case, just as the 1985 council did 40 years ago.

Will Folly Remain Folly?

Will Folly remain a residential community with some rentals, or become a rental community with some residents?

I wish I could give you a definitive answer. I am heartened by the dedication of all the people who succeeded in attaining that successful binding referendum. Hopefully, the tide has been turned toward love of community and the permanent resident population will once again defend itself if it needs to.

But powerful forces are aligned to make sure that commercial profit trumps quality of life. As citizens, we have to wake from our dream that our quality of life is a product of debate *within* the community, because with the popularity and growth that our area is experiencing, dark money has arrived. Greed doesn't care about quality of life or whether or not the heart of the community survives.

Like the citizens of 1984, we need to roll up our sleeves and get to work. Folly's citizens will have to be willing to run for office and always insist that our representatives protect a strong and vibrant permanent population.

I choose to believe we will.

As proof that "it is never over until its over," four councilmembers have expressed an interest in introducing legislation at the council's April 11, 2023 meeting that dismantles the heart of the ordinance that capped investor-owned short-term rentals (ISTRs).

The battle continues. Please follow the Facebook page "Remaining Folly" to stay abreast of the details of the struggle.

Epilogue

I grew up in a time when corporal punishment of children was not uncommon. I was occasionally on the receiving end of that form of discipline, but it didn't happen often because I was more easily influenced by the evidence of displeasure than by physical punishment. I was a pleaser and a peacemaker. That child grew into a similarly disposed adult.

When I think back on the events described in this history, they seem surreal. How in the world did I stay in a position so at odds with my basic personality? How did I continue to persevere against the vitriol and aggression that my actions precipitated?

I learned that when you are committed to an action you believe in and are a part of a group of like-minded individuals, whether someone likes you is no longer important. As a team, we were stronger and more resilient than we ever could have been as individuals. We were, in effect, brothers and sisters in arms. Perhaps, as Paulo Coelho reminds us in *The Alchemist*, "When you want something, all the universe conspires in helping you to achieve it."

Every commitment has a price. The mistake I made was forgetting one of the most important rules of success—to maintain a balance in one's life. I let my political commitments take precedence over everything else, including my marriage.

I realigned my priorities, but the damage I did to my marriage in its formative years did not allow for healing. In 1997, eight years after my resignation, Nancy and I divorced after twelve years of marriage. Obsessions are expensive; debts will be paid.

I drifted until one day in the fall of 1998 when I got a call from Jim Booth, a local artist and high school friend. "Richard," he said, "I want you to meet some people."

"I appreciate that," I responded. "Who are they?"

"A group of people who are trying to save the Morris Island Lighthouse. I think you'd be a good team member."

I paused for a second. "I really appreciate it," I said, "but the last thing I need right now is to get involved with a group of people dealing with a controversy."

Nonetheless, he was persistent. "This is the most dedicated group of people you could ever hope to find, and you should meet them. I'll tell you what. Go with me to one meeting. If you aren't totally impressed, you can disappear, and I'll never say another word about it. I promise."

I finally agreed.

After my first "Save The Light" meeting, I was completely on board. Jim was right. They were a wonderful group of people. For 22 years now, I have been blessed to be among their number.

The people I have met through "Save The Light" and the Morris Island Lighthouse itself are dear to my heart. Had I known how much work would be involved in making the progress we've made, though, I might never have gotten involved. Had I known how many great people I would meet and all the good times we would share while doing the work, I would have started sooner. "Save the Light" restored my faith in grassroots service.

In 2006, I combined my dental practice with Dr. Robert Beall's and enjoyed my association with him and our wonderful staff until my retirement from dentistry in 2016 after 44 years.

In 2009, ten years after joining "Save The Light," I had the good fortune to meet Karen Lovelace. We recently celebrated our 12th wedding anniversary. I am blessed beyond description to know the love of Karen, her three children, my daughter, and our combined eight grandchildren.

Now I travel with Karen, conduct dolphin tours, enjoy children and grandchildren, explore photography and music, maintain my boat, stay involved in Folly politics and lately, work on this book about Folly's history.

I am a fortunate man.

Richard L. Beck, DMD
Folly City Councilman: 1978–1982
Mayor: 1982–1989

Appendix

Resources

In writing this book, I depended on a number of resources.

I depended heavily on Google research and archived articles in what was then the *News and Courier* for accurate dates and general content. They used to follow and report on the events unfolding on Folly very carefully. Fortunately, Marlene Estridge kept a city scrapbook of any mention of Folly in the media through almost all of the period of time that I was in office.

Dinos Liollio was kind enough to make the research that he did on Folly for his master's degree available to me.

James Hagy's *The Folly Beach Book* (ISBN 978-1-57510-46-0) is a wonderful pictorial review of the history of Folly Beach. You should find it.

I kept an extensive file of official correspondence and a great many photographs of this time period.

I kept copies of planning documents, workshop and panel conclusions, and official findings of the studies by the U.S. Army Corps of Engineers.

I was able to talk to many of the people involved or their partners to keep the facts straight and add color and texture.

And then there is my memory, which I found was the least reliable source and the one I had to check most carefully against other resources.

Cast of Characters

It takes a lot of work for a citizenry to triumph over an unenlightened city council. The following individuals, arranged in no particular order, made the victories possible. There are many others that I do not recall as clearly. For that, I apologize.

PAUL AND CAROLYN SHELTON – Paul and Carolyn could be the subject of a great short story. Longtime realtors on Folly, they were completely dedicated to qualitative improvements and common sense. They had two very different personalities and in the midst of heated discussions, I often felt that, if you didn't know that they were married, you wouldn't think they knew each other at all. Paul made his points with bombast and petulant insistence; Carolyn would listen carefully and offer thoughtful, gentle and wise council. Often speaking last, she would bring closure to contentious discussions. Whenever I think of Carolyn, I am reminded that we ultimately live on through what we teach each other about love.

TOM AND MARIANNE READ – Tom and Marianne were "Old Folly" to the core. They were always willing to help. You name it and they would do it. They both enjoyed speaking truth to power. Marianne went on to serve on the seminal council of 1986. For many years, Tom's father ran a notion shop and Tom and Marianne ran Read Brother's Stereo in the building that Tom's grandfather built at the SW corner of Spring and King streets.

WES AND FRANCES MURPHY – Wes and Frances ran the Turtle Corner Grocery in the building that Follywood occupies in 2023. They lived across the street from me on East Ashley and were great neighbors. For 10 years after I moved to Folly, I was single, and probably ate more meals at Frances's table than at my own. Wes always met me with a whiskey on the rocks in his hand.

The Murphys were so good for the island and loved it so dearly. Turtle Corner became the de facto headquarters of the FIRA movement for protection of the island's way of life. I honestly don't know how they got any business done. They are both gone now. Their legacy is significant.

BERT KETCHAM – Bert was gruff and didn't suffer fools well. If you asked him what time it was, he would teach you how to build a clock. His wife Jo was much softer. Jo was good natured, a good listener and usually punctuated her comments with a short little giggle. Together they were unwavering and well-respected supporters of FIRA. Bert served as election commissioner for much of this period. It was comforting to know that someone with his integrity was at that helm.

JOHN AND JUDY MANZI – John and Judy have been my friends since John asked me if I wanted to go have a beer after a City Council meeting in May of 1978. John and Judy have also been good friends of the Island. John and Dr. Margaret Davison - second director of the Sea Grant Consortium - put together the National Science Foundation grant that funded the Workshop on Erosion Abatement in 1979. That symposium was the springboard for our successful acquisition of a Corps of Engineers Section 1-11 and the fifty - year commitment on the part of the U. S. Army Corps of Engineers to keep Folly renourished. Smart, good humored, energetic, and excellent strategists, I can't imagine success without John and Judy.

BOB AND FLO STOERTZ – Bob and Flo were pillars of the movement. They were both chemical engineers. Bob was also a photographic enthusiast. They had traveled the world and truly loved the Folly we knew at that time. They were both colorful. Bob was quiet but quick and...well...you just didn't want to cross Flo. They were mean motor scooters when they believed that their lifestyle was threatened. Flo became the spokesman for FIRA and often appeared at City Council meetings to give them a tongue lashing over what FIRA saw as their lack of concern for the community.

OSCAR AND DEE OAKES – Oscar and Dee were also across the street neighbors of mine. They owned the two buildings on the north side of the Baptist church as well as a tool company in the Rock Hill area. They offered great support to FIRA and me during this time period but ended up working against me on the Dry Stack Marina issue.

FRANK AND LEE ROEBER – Frank and Lee were also my neighbors and were solid supporters of FIRA. They were full of Yankee brashness and loud laughter. Being from a part of the country that knew a thing or two about the corruptive effect of high-density development, they could speak about such things with conviction and did so without hesitation. Later they attempted to turn what is now the public boat landing at the foot of the bridge into a large dry stack storage facility. We came to blows over that but recovered and remained friends.

LARRY AND JERRI RIDGEWAY – Larry and Jerri were the owners of Florence Paper Co. (AMSPAC) and ran it from their office in what is currently the Bounty Bar on Center Street (the old bingo parlor of the fifties). I served on city council with Larry and counted him a dear friend and traveling companion. I wish I could get a nickel for every Larry story I could tell. Larry was ferocious and articulate. Jerri's smile promised that there was plenty of strength behind it. Francis Wilborn would not sit next to Larry in city council meetings because he intimidated her so much. He was tough, smart, fierce, and impatient. Larry was the muscle in the movement. Larry organized the first city-wide festival: The Folly Beach Reunion in 1983. Without him, saving the residential quality of life on Folly may well have never happened.

NANCY CARTER – Although her frame was diminutive, Nancy radiated the confidence of a giant. Her wry sense of humor was merciless and irreverent. She and her son Mark were always willing to tackle whatever was required to preserve the Folly that they so loved, and to do so with gusto.

ROGERS AND RITA OGLESBY – Rogers and Rita were the anchors of the FIRA movement. Rogers was an accomplished artist in several mediums, a manager for GE, an excellent planner, and an effective political cartoonist. Rita is an accountant. They loved this beach and what it could be. As long as Rogers was able, he fought for intelligent, thoughtful and responsible government. As the organizer and driving force behind FIRA, we simply would have had zero chance of success if Rogers hadn't been the visionary leader that he was. No one worked harder or more effectively for the best interests of Folly in the '70s and '80s than did Rogers and Rita Oglesby. Without Rogers, I can't imagine our history being what it is. In many ways, Rogers IS the story.

BEN PEEPLES – Ben served as Folly's attorney for 40 years It is difficult to overstate just how much he contributed to Folly. I was fortunate to be able to call on him for political as well as personal advice. In the battle that surrounded FIRA's efforts, he somehow found a way to do what was ethically correct while also making sure that FIRA was treated fairly. It was not an easy thing to do. Folly owes Ben a debt of gratitude on many fronts.

BILL LEE – Bill was already involved in Folly politics when I came on council. He   was the chairman of both the first erosion committee and the planning and zoning board in the late '70s. He was known as "Board a Day Bill" for his attempt to build a multistory house in the 1500 block of East Ashley all by himself. I would stop by when I saw him working and enjoyed sitting and talking to him. He was a single man and had two sons from a previous marriage. He struck me as one of the most secure and happy people I've ever met. I had never married at the time, and he always reminded me of my need to find a wife and have children. He loved his boys. It was a spiritual pleasure to get to know Bill. I can still see his smile today.

CLIFF HARVEY AND BRIAN PORTER – Cliff and Brian (who has since passed) are among the most willing and capable public servants to have ever served Folly. When Wallace Benson resigned as police and fire chief, they stepped right into the breach, negotiated our mutual aid pact with James Island and patiently educated the volunteers and newly-hired police officers in the art of firefighting. They also served as reserve officers and volunteer firemen for too many years to count.

U.S. SENATOR ERNEST F. (FRITZ) HOLLINGS – Fritz Hollings was a friend to Folly before I met him. He worked tirelessly to bring to bear whatever influence he could, as we were trying to navigate the U.S. Army Corps of Engineer bureaucracy. Senator Hollings' help is what allowed us access to the Corps data before it was published so that we could confer with them and reach mutually agreed upon conclusions before pride of publication could get in the way. When Hugo hit (September 1989), it was Senator Hollings who helped Mayor Linville secure the money for Folly's first re-nourishment project utilizing our successful Section 1-11 review in June of 1992.

DR. MARGARET DAVIDSON – Dr. Davidson followed Dr. John Armstrong as second head of the South Carolina Sea Grant Consortium. Margaret was smart, funny, scarily capable, and so excitable about planning and educating about all things coastal, that she forced good things to happen all around her. A consummate networker, she got me funding for an attempt at executing an optimum population revamp of Folly's zoning called an Island Plan.

Very early on, she helped me get into venues as a speaker so that I could talk about beachfront management issues to a wide audience, at a time when there was no consensus that there was a beachfront problem at all. She went on the be the founding director of NOAA's Coastal Resource Center. The awards that she amassed and the good she did for common sense coastal stewardship are just too numerous to mention. She was something else.

MARLENE ESTRIDGE – Marlene was and still is one of the most beloved people on Folly Island. Her husband Marvin was involved in the political scene at Folly for many years until his death in 1981.

Marlene took over the management of the front office of the city in 1980 and is still there today—with her loving smile and limitless knowledge of the who, what, when, and where of Folly. She always strikes me as the beating heart of Folly. Her wisdom and assistance were and still are an incomparable blessing to everyone whose life she touches.

WAYNE HEMBREE – Wayne was a field deputy for the South Carolina Employment Securities Commission. Without his service on city council from 1984–1988, we would have never been successful. Ten people ran for office to fill three seats the year he, John, and Elliot were elected. If anyone of those ten besides John and Wayne would have been elected, I am sure that the history of Folly would be quite different. He was respected in the community for his straightforward, pull - no - punches attitude. He was a stalwart, good tempered soldier when the going got tough.

HARRIET McCUTCHEN – Harriet was an active community organizer that was very instrumental in getting FIRA up and running. Harriet was always ready to write, call, copy, raise money, or anything else that FIRA required for success. After Rogers was elected to council, and Oscar Oakes resigned, she became the president of FIRA and helped me in coordinating our unfortunately unsuccessful attempt to get the "Island Plan" accepted and passed. She was a tireless worker for the island's better interests.

GEORGE TITTLE, JR – George came to Folly after a couple of failed attempts to find a police chief following Wallace Benson's resignation. He, his wife Marty, and I enjoyed our association.

Folly had very limited resources early on. George took the concept of public safety, first implemented by Jack Wilbanks, and made it function. He vastly improved the efficiency of fire/police service on the island. It takes a good leader to make that concept work and George was up to the task. He was laid back but firm, funny but professional. He had the most amazing crooked smile that would warm anyone's heart. His son Paul has followed in his father's footsteps as an excellent police officer. George's cool leadership was absolutely vital to turning Folly's police force into a modern effective service.

U.S. REPRESENTATIVE ARTHUR RAVENEL JR. AND DANA BEACH – Both of these individuals played a big role in keeping the Corps on tract after the Section 1-11 commitment was obtained. They effectively made sure that the federal money remained in the budget so that the Corps' commitment became a reality.

ERIC OLSEN, PE – Eric was the coastal engineer who served as Folly's consultant in our effort to get the U.S. Army Corps of Engineers to take responsibility for the erosion caused by the Charleston harbor jetties. He did an outstanding job. Navigating that path successfully takes unimpeachable knowledge, a calm demeanor, and the soul of a diplomat. He was able to lay out the facts that supported our claim and dispute the incorrect conclusions of the Corps with a grace and persistence that ultimately led the Corps to agree to a fifty-year commitment to keep Folly's beach renourished. Eric, more than any other person, deserves the credit for the healthy beach you find at Folly today.

JOHN MCFARLAND – John is my new hero. When City Council refused to even debate limiting Investment Short-Term Rentals (ISTRs) in June of 2021, John formed Save Folly's Future and all but singlehandedly initiated, financed and manned the effort to put an ordinance before council to limit ISTRS via the initiative and referendum component of the Home Rule Act.

Just as in 1984, when Rogers Oglesby spearheaded a similar effort, a single citizen made it possible for the citizens of Folly to use "initiative and referendum" to defend their right to a sustainable community.

ANN PEETS AND KRISTEN KAPPEL – Ann and Kristen took on the task of creating a marketing and communications strategy for FRA. They focused on providing a consistent, clear, and truthful source of information fact checked against multiple sources to keep the debate honest. They also debunked daily distortions and misinformation presented by FU. Their honest, yet hard-hitting multimedia campaign, and door-to-door discussions was a successful one with over 1,200 voters coming out and helping to secure a win for the Residents of Folly.

On behalf of all the citizens to come that will benefit from their leadership, I would like to thank John, Ann, Kristen and all those who are not mentioned for their commitment to ensuring that Folly remains a place that people can call home.

Made in the USA
Columbia, SC
29 May 2023